WILLIAM KELLY OF PORTRANE

Forgotten Hero of The Famine and Land War

GERARD RONAN

libraries.
fingal.ie

ISBN: 9781999973827
ISBN-13: 978-1999973827

Cover Image: Detail from Winter Work, 1883-4, by Sir George Clausen. Courtesy of Tate Images.

Also by Gerard Ronan

The Irish Zorro
The Round Towers of Fingal
Sophia Parnell Evans – Feminism, Politics
and Farming in 19th Century Portrane
Margaret Evans – Poet of Portrane

For Bríd & Kevin

CONTENTS

‘He who writes the history of Ireland’s social condition and progress, during the dark days to which we refer, will leave his task unfinished if he omits from his pages the name of William Kelly.’

The Farmer’s Gazette, August 1856.

ACKNOWLEDGEMENTS

I owe particular thanks to Gregory O'Connor, archivist at the National Archives in Dublin for his guidance and patience, and to the staff of the Document Supply Service of the National Library of Australia who supplied me with a copy of Kelly's *Essay on Villa Farms.* I am also especially grateful to Gordon Henderson for the guided tour and aerial photographs of William Kelly's former home at Middlefield and permission to photograph it.

My thanks also to Damian Murphy at the National Inventory of Architectural Heritage for his photographs of the Bannow Farm School, and to Lynn Brady, Resident Genealogist at the Glasnevin Cemetery Museum for her assistance in finding the graves and attempting to unravel the mystery of Mary Jane's exhumation. I am grateful also to Alan McCann for his review of the agricultural elements, to Stephen Rice for his thoughtful comments and encouragement, and to the staff of the General Register Office who helped me find the death certificates.

Special thanks are also due to Helen O'Donnell, and to Fingal County Council, without whose assistance this book would not have been published. Last, but not least, I owe a debt of gratitude to my wife, Cliona, and my daughter, Eleanor, for their eternal forbearance and support.

INTRODUCTION

ONE SULTRY EVENING in September 1845, suffragette and animal rights campaigner, Frances Power Cobbe, was travelling to seven o'clock dinner at the home of her 'dear friend', Mrs Sophia Evans of Portrane. As her coach passed a field of potatoes, she could not help but remark on the exceptionally leafy display. A bumper crop seemed likely. Indeed, bumper crops had been a regular occurrence since Mrs Evans hired William Kelly as her steward.

Four hours later, as the coach in which she and six other passengers were travelling returned to Newbridge House, one of her young companions caught a whiff of a dreadful smell wafting from the very same field. 'Something has happened to those potatoes,' she remarked, 'they do not smell at all as they did when we passed them on our way out.' They could not have known it at the time, but they had witnessed the birth of a catastrophe.

It had been an unusually wet and humid summer. No amount of barometer tapping could force the needle from *Rain* and the *phytophthora infestans* fungus had enjoyed perfect conditions for reproduction. Spores that developed on the undersides of the leaves had been washed by persistent rain into the soil, where they had proceeded to infect the tubers. When the farmers went to dig them up, all they found was a black sticky mess.

That potato field, in which Frances and her dinner companions first noticed the blight, belonged, like most of the fields around Portrane House, to the aforementioned Mrs Evans, whose land steward was the talented and visionary agriculturalist, William Kelly. Before he came to work at Portrane, Kelly was already the author of a published work, *An essay on the general management of Villa Farms.* It had been published in 1836.

Kelly was unable to save his potatoes. In all of Fingal, only those that grew in the sandy seaweed-manured fields of The Burrow were spared. The microscopic spores, normally killed by cold weather, could travel for miles on the wind and the fungus was capable of reproducing so rapidly that an entire field of potatoes could be devastated in hours. Once it had taken hold there was little that anyone could do. Between September and October 1845, it ruined between a third and a half of the island's potato crop.

As botanical experts debated whether the blight was a symptom or a cause of the rotting potatoes, William Kelly decided that the cause was irrelevant. What mattered was that the potato crop had been proven vulnerable. The potential consequences of a repeat were unthinkable, especially for that part of the population that was so totally dependent on it.

The only practicable solution, Kelly believed, was to find some means of reducing the dependence of small farmers on the potato without increasing the financial burden on their families. He had kept up with all the latest European advances in science and agriculture and had already travelled part of the way towards a solution in the methods he had been introducing for five years now at Portrane.

It was important to act quickly, but in Dublin Castle officials dithered. Afraid that too few seed potatoes might be sown for the following year, officials failed to discourage farmers from cutting away the rotten parts of the tubers and storing what was left for planting the following year. The spores, in consequence, overwintered and spread even further when the infected tubers were re-planted. By August 1846, the entire country was in the grip of a famine.

The small tenant farmers of 19th century Ireland had come to rely almost exclusively on the potato for food and the failure of the crop, as Kelly had anticipated, brought widespread malnutrition and disease. Strictly speaking there was no 'famine'. The word implies a shortage of food. Ireland, however, was producing a surplus; a surplus that was being sent daily, and under armed guard, to England, where it was desperately needed to feed the foot-soldiers of the Industrial Revolution. The cost of *this* food, however, lay beyond the purse of the average Irish peasant, for whom there was no affordable alternative to the potato.

With his reputation so recently enhanced by his transformation of the Evans estate, Kelly assumed, somewhat optimistically, that all it would take to get the small farmers of Ireland to listen to him, would be to provide them with a detailed proof and accurate costings of his proven methods of crop rotation. Lessons had been learned locally from his record-breaking yields and he had the data to prove it. As the land steward for the Evans estate he'd had a great deal of influence over his tenants and, whether through example or gentle persuasion, his innovations had taken root and allowed the famine to bypass Portrane.

Indeed Kelly's experimental and 'statistical'

approach to farming would prove so successful that over the course of the famine, the population of the Portrane peninsula would manage to significantly buck the national trend. No one, not one single person, would die there from starvation, and only a handful would be forced to emigrate.

Throughout the adjacent agricultural areas of north County Dublin, in the period between the census of 1841 and that of 1851, the population would fall by between twelve and twenty per cent. On the Portrane peninsula, by way of contrast, it would fall by just 0.8%. Consider that figure for a moment. At a time of famine, disease, evictions and high emigration, the population of the Portrane peninsula would drop by just ten people in ten years.

<table>
<tr><th colspan="4">Population Decline 1841-1851</th></tr>
<tr><th>Area</th><th>Year</th><th>Population</th><th>%Fall</th></tr>
<tr><td rowspan="2">Greater Lusk</td><td>1841</td><td>4893</td><td rowspan="2">12%</td></tr>
<tr><td>1851</td><td>4282</td></tr>
<tr><td rowspan="2">Greater Swords</td><td>1841</td><td>3633</td><td rowspan="2">18%</td></tr>
<tr><td>1851</td><td>2962</td></tr>
<tr><td rowspan="2">Kilsallaghan</td><td>1841</td><td>1312</td><td rowspan="2">20%</td></tr>
<tr><td>1851</td><td>1052</td></tr>
<tr><td rowspan="2">Ballyboghill</td><td>1841</td><td>842</td><td rowspan="2">16%</td></tr>
<tr><td>1851</td><td>705</td></tr>
<tr><td rowspan="2">Greater Balbriggan</td><td>1841</td><td>4881</td><td rowspan="2">20%</td></tr>
<tr><td>1851</td><td>3864</td></tr>
<tr><td rowspan="2">Donabate/Portrane</td><td>1841</td><td>1170</td><td rowspan="2">< 1%</td></tr>
<tr><td>1851</td><td>1160</td></tr>
</table>

There were, of course, other possible factors involved. The blight had failed to take a firm hold on the sandy, windswept, and seaweed-soaked soil of The Burrow, and there was, at least initially, a plentiful supply of shellfish on the Rogerstown estuary. But similar resources had also been available to the people on the Lusk side of the Rogerstown Estuary, where the population dropped by 12%. Truth be told, there was only so much shellfish to go around, and the tiny potato fields of The Burrow could not generate enough of a surplus to compensate for losses elsewhere.

Something different was obviously happening in Portrane. Labour intensive farming was proving not just productive, but profitable. Small farmers were not going hungry, nor were they falling prey in any great numbers to disease. Farm labourers were being kept gainfully employed, at least during the usual seasons, and even the ragged children of the poor were being fed and educated.

Reports of Kelly's bumper crop yields saw curiosity in Sophia Evans' estate explode. It bolstered her personal reputation as a liberal and charitable landlady, and her land steward's reputation as a skilled and innovative agriculturalist. Between 1846 and 1849, Kelly's advice on resource management, crop rotation, and waste recycling became a widely quoted and much published public resource. Pamphlets, books, newspapers, and journals on both sides of the Atlantic began to reference his work. For a short time, he was perhaps the most famous farmer in Ireland. A method of green crop cultivation would even be named after him.

So, what exactly was going on at Portrane? Why, with the spectre of *Black '47* hovering ominously over the country at large, did the Irish Farmers' Association ask forty-year-old William Kelly to urgently publish what was essentially a survival guide for small farmers? What was so revolutionary about his approach to farming that, just two years after its publication, a Canadian agricultural journal would be quoting from the *fifth* edition of his book and recommending his methods to Canadian farmers? What was it about William Kelly that inspired such confidence in his labourers, tenant farmers, and political colleagues? And how did this self-deprecating agricultural empiricist come to find himself at the heart of the tenants' rights, Home Rule, and Land League movements at the very moment of their inceptions?

In the immediate aftermath of the famine, those best placed to judge such matters considered William Kelly something of a visionary and a trailblazer. In 1856, a decade before he took his first tentative steps into the world of politics and agrarian activism, *The Farmer's Gazette* wrote:

'He who writes the history of Ireland's social condition and progress, during the dark days to which we refer, will leave his task unfinished if he omits from his pages the name of William Kelly'.

Twelve years later an agricultural correspondent of the Dublin Evening Post would describe Kelly as

'...one of the distinguished professional agriculturists in Great Britain or Ireland and one of the most successful practical farmers of the present time.'

So how is it, indeed *why* is it, that today, even on the peninsula where he spent most of his adult life and where his many public services would have had the greatest impact, the name of William Kelly of Portrane has been almost entirely forgotten?

THE BANNOW FARM SCHOOL

The Bannow Farm School. Photo courtesy of The National Inventory of Architectural Heritage.

THE STORY OF the Bannow Farm School, like that of William Kelly, is a story largely lost to history. When it first opened in 1821, it marked the beginning of vocational education in Ireland, preceding the Mechanics' Institute in Dublin by almost three years. In its essence, it was a simple agricultural school. But look a little closer and you will find that Bannow was so much more than that.

Located at Vernegly, just 2km from the shores of Bannow Bay, on the east side of the Hook Peninsula, the two-storey farmhouse that housed the Bannow Farm School was home to young men of disparate social backgrounds. They had come together in an educational experiment as curious and odd in the eyes of the local population as the whales that, once in a generation, would strand themselves on the sands of Bannow Bay.

Funded partly by a grant from Charles Talbot, the Lord Lieutenant of Ireland, it was established on forty acres of land donated by local landlord, Thomas Boyse (or Boyce, depending on which source you read). The school's founder, the Rev. William Hickey, was the local Anglican vicar and students from any part of the country were accepted, 'no matter how poor their physical or intellectual development'. The school's first roll call counted nineteen. Most were the sons of local farmers. A few, however, had travelled from more distant parishes, amongst them a schoolboy from County Monaghan by the name of William Kelly.

At Bannow Kelly shared a dormitory with local boys who ranged in age from thirteen to twenty. Most of them already knew each other. They spoke with the same local accent, shared private jokes, and referenced unfamiliar personalities. *His* northern lilt marked him as an outsider. He was just fifteen; still young enough to miss his mother.

Elizabeth Kelly was forty-five when she gave birth to William; sixty when she placed him as a boarder at Bannow. Rapidly approaching that time when she would be wholly dependent upon her child to support her in her old age, his enrolment represented an investment in both their futures. William was her last, and possibly only, son. He was also her last, and possibly only, hope. From the very start, there was an imperative to succeed.

I could only find one Elizabeth Kelly from Monaghan who would have been sixty years of age in 1821, the year that William enrolled at Bannow. She lived in Drummond Etra and worked as a cook for a Mr Humphrey Evatt. Evatt was the land agent of Evelyn John Shirley, an 'indulgent landlord who admitted tenant right on his property to the fullest extent.'

We know precious little about this intensely private household. When the census agent called to the Evatt cottage in 1821, he was swiftly run off the property by Evatt, who refused to divulge the ages of anyone in his family. The agent made no mention of a William Kelly or, for that matter, of any Mr Kelly. But, by his own admission, he had not been present long enough to complete his enquiries and it is possible that William had by then already left for Bannow.

Humphrey Evatt was known as a kind and generous man. It would have been entirely consistent with his character to sponsor the son of an employee to be educated as a land agent like himself, especially if that child had shown a real head for figures and a natural aptitude for agriculture. Evatt was also known to be sympathetic to the plight of Catholics and to be on very friendly terms with the parish priest of Carrickmacross, the Rev. President Reilly.

There is, however, no evidence whatsoever to link Evatt to the sponsorship of William's education other than the coincidence of his personal cook happening to have had the right name, age and county to have been William's mother, and the fact that Evatt, too, was employed in the same profession that William Kelly had been apprenticed to learn. But whatever the source, it is unlikely that William Kelly arrived at Bannow without the aid of some form of patronage.

At Bannow, William Kelly would rise each day at six, spend an hour and a half at manual work on the farm, then take breakfast at eight (usually porridge and milk). From nine till one he would work on the farm with half of the boys while the other half attended classes inside. If attending classes in the morning, he would work on the farm in the afternoons.

Dinner each day was from one 'till two and consisted of potatoes and milk. Occasionally a treat of bread and soup would grace the table. Twice a week, on Thursdays and Sundays, he would be given meat and vegetables. By the standards of the time, he was being well fed. The boys had not been apprenticed to provide cheap labour. Bannow was a *bona fide* college.

Hickey attached great importance to the skills of ploughmanship and gardening, but also believed in developing his students' abilities in mental arithmetic; a commonplace of vocational education at the time. A report for The Farming Society declared results in this subject at Bannow to be 'scarcely equalled in any other school'. Work was all about equations; life always about balance.

Beyond arithmetic, the academic curriculum was broad: reading, writing, mensuration (geometry), surveying, 'the mechanic powers', agricultural chemistry, crop rotation, and gardening, with the study of botany added after the first year. All of these, Kelly studied under the instruction of a certain Mr Edwards. Despite the young age of the students, there was no time for frivolous games or recreation. To the Rev. William Hickey, farm work *was* relaxation.

Practical instruction took place in the fields. It consisted of ploughing, sowing, reaping, and the various operations of the farm. Taught by an anonymous Scottish land steward according to the 'Scotch System' of land management, it was heavily influenced by the writings of Sir John Sinclair of Ulbster, the first person to coin the word 'statistics'. In the years to come, Sinclair's approach to the economic management of farms would prove a major influence on William Kelly's published works, and his lifelong reverence of 'statistics'.

As befitted a working farm, daily routine varied according to season and weather. More hours were allocated to indoor study during the winter, when there was less work to be done outside, and less during the summer, when the hours of labour were long. In such respects, the Bannow Farm School was offering bog-standard agricultural apprenticeships, that many of the local farmers felt convinced could be better learnt at home from their Irish elders. But, in other ways, the school was thoroughly unique.

Education at Bannow was flexible and followed the abilities of the children, who were generally permitted to learn at their own pace. Upon enrolment, each student would be assessed regarding his character and interests, and his independent activities watched as closely as his performance in the classroom. Teachers would then guide him towards subjects that would excite him as an individual.

From the very start, the emphasis was on fostering a lifelong love of learning rather than turning out 'magazines of knowledge'. Through the cultivation of conscience, understanding, and judgement, the school endeavoured to prepare its students for what it called the 'business of life'.

If there was any single period in William Kelly's life that could truly be said to have been formative, it was the five years he spent here under Hickey's benevolent mentorship. In both his private and his public life, he would become a flattering reflection of everything the school and, indeed, its founder, had stood for. But the credit did not belong to Hickey alone. In establishing the school, Hickey had merely been following a path first trodden by another original thinker. His name was Philip von Fellenberg.

In the early years of the nineteenth century, the pernicious postulates of the Protestant Ascendancy had been neatly encapsulated in a verse of a hugely popular and highly sanctimonious Sunday School hymn for infants, *All Things Bright and Beautiful*:

The rich man in his castle,
The poor man at the gate,
God made them high and lowly,
And ordered their estate.

Abhorrent to the modern eye, it reflected a deeply held belief that in doing little to help the poor, the rich were simply acting in accordance with God's plan and encouraging them to help themselves. Most educational systems at that time reflected this kind of moral rhetoric, effectively locking the children of the poor into their allotted station in life.

Within this narrow mindset, however, there was still room for imaginative thought. Certain liberal-minded individuals had, indeed, already begun to search for alternative models. They found what they were seeking, or so it seemed at the time, in the school of a famous Swiss educationalist.

Philip von Fellenberg believed that Divine Wisdom had divided society into three classes: those born to rule (i.e. the nobility and the wealthy), the middling, and those born to obey (the poor). In his mixture of manual and formal education, he believed he had discovered a tool by which the highest and lowest classes could be educated in tandem. Within this model, the upper classes would develop a sense of responsibility and sympathy for the poor, and the lower classes would better prepare themselves for the 'station in which Providence had placed them'.

In 1799, Fellenberg purchased the estate of Hofwyl, near Bern, with a dream of making agriculture the basis of this system. Labour, according to Fellenberg, was the great moraliser of man, and agriculture, the type of labour most uniquely suited to welding the lower and upper classes in mutual respect. The initial reaction to his school was ridicule. But he made it work, and word spread. Princes and paupers began to flock to Hofwyl to study agriculture and to profit from the high moral training that he had embedded in his system. When word of his experiment reached England, the Liberal MP and anti-slavery campaigner, Henry Brougham, decided to travel to Switzerland to judge for himself. He spent three months at Hofwyl in 1818.

On his return to London, Brougham documented his conclusions in two articles written for the *Edinburgh Review.* These subsequently formed the basis of a pamphlet, *The State of the Poor in Ireland,* published in 1820 by old Cantabrigian, William Hickey, the thirty-two-year-old Anglican Vicar of Bannow, in County Wexford.

Inspired by Fellenberg's ideals, Hickey founded a 'Farm School' loosely based on the Fellenberg model. His ambition, from the outset, was to educate the sons of farmers 'with a view to their becoming stewards, gardeners, practical farmers on their own account, or masters for other schools.' Unlike Fellenberg, however, Hickey saw education as a path, for those who possessed the necessary talent, to both moral improvement *and* social advancement.

Hickey was determined that the school should be ecumenical in nature, something that was not easily achieved given the social and political situation of the time. Nevertheless, despite local suspicions of proselytism, he managed to navigate the doctrinal differences and gain the unlikely support of the local Catholic clergy. Catholic and Protestant students took religious instruction separately, Hickey taking care of the Protestants, and the local Parish Priest the Catholics.

Nevertheless, the students still prayed together in the evenings and took joint lessons in piety and moral behaviour from Hickey, who acted as the school's 'Moral Master'. Such was the general tone of religiosity, that students would often refer to the school as the 'seminary'. A report to the Royal Dublin Society in 1827 noted that:

'It is a matter of heart-felt satisfaction that Protestants and Catholics, pupils, tradesmen and servants, have been most cordially associated without ... the least compromise of principle or any degree of indifference on the subject of religion'.

At the same time as he was formulating his ideas for the farm school, Hickey also established the South Wexford Agricultural Society, the first society of its kind anywhere in Ireland. In the context of William Kelly's later life this, too, would have a significant impact, for it was through the efforts of this society that Hickey managed to introduce the mangelwurzel plant to Wexford.

Such was the opposition to the introduction of this beet-like plant that Hickey's agricultural society had to offer premiums to induce some of the local farmers to plant it. Even then the experiment was very nearly scuppered by the decision of the local bishop to impose a tithe upon its cultivation. In later years it would be Kelly's innovative usage of this plant that would help to save many lives on the Portrane peninsula during the early years of the famine.

At Bannow, William Kelly was not just compelled to attend formal classes, but encouraged to indulge in those activities to which he felt individually drawn. Some of his fellow students would opt to specialise as educators, some as ploughmen and others as gardeners and tillage farmers. Kelly was very much in the latter group, though this may have had something, at least initially, to do with his age.

Despite the unique educational opportunity that Hickey was offering, the biggest problem facing the school in its initial years was the reluctance of local farmers to lose experienced farmhands. As a result, Hickey had to hire labourers to do much of the heavy work, such as draining, ditching, and building. The ongoing expense would eventually bankrupt the school.

The inexpensive general education, on the other hand, *did* encourage parents to send their younger children, many at an age when their bodies were simply too immature to handle the more physical aspects of farming. At fifteen Kelly was too young to take a man's place at the plough and draw a straight furrow. He was not, however, too young to dig potatoes. Approaching his practical lessons with the same scientific seriousness that he approached his academic classes he thrived in the fields and found his vocation at the end of a spade.

From the outset, money was a problem. Neither the land nor its physically immature students could produce enough crops to sustain the school and Hickey was soon forced to rely almost exclusively upon fees and charitable donations. Boarders initially paid from four to six guineas a year, depending on personal circumstances. By 1824, however, rising costs had forced Hickey to confine admittance to new entrants who could pay a single payment of thirty guineas in advance of their five-year apprenticeship.

And it wasn't just the school that was impoverished. The soil, too, was poor. Consisting of just forty acres of waterlogged soil, Bannow wasn't Hofwyl. If there was to be a farm at all, the land needed to be drained, reclaimed, and cultivated.

In observing and helping in this transformative drainage and land reclamation, Kelly learnt invaluable lessons that he would later put into extensive use at Portrane. Indeed, so successful were the land reclamation efforts at Bannow that, just three years after the school had opened, a report to a parliamentary committee would describe the land as having been miraculously transformed into productive pasture on which 'lucerne, vetches, rape, peas and mangelwurzel' were being grown.

The school, alas, would not be given time to profitably exploit the improvements. In 1826, as was always likely to happen to a talented cleric, the Rev. William Hickey was promoted to a larger parish. By that time, many of the boys had already been moved to Bessmount, near Enniscorthy, to see out the remainder of their apprenticeships on a working estate. At Bessmount, Kelly's education would be completed with the occasional assistance of a new mentor, the Rev. Richard Radcliffe, an innovative and respected agriculturalist. Radcliffe would regularly invite students from the Bannow school onto his farm at the side of Vinegar Hill to study and learn the means by which he had overcome the challenge of farming on difficult ground. His influence on Kelly would be profound.

Without Hickey's unique commitment and talent for fundraising, the Bannow Farm School finally closed its doors in 1826. By this time, with the summer harvest already in at Bessmount, William Kelly had graduated and returned to Monaghan. His childhood was over. It was time to find employment.

From a roll of twenty-eight pupils, the Bannow Farm School's unconventional system of education managed to produce some decent farmers and ploughmen, a couple of agricultural teachers, and a couple of land stewards. Their education prepared them well for their chosen careers, but it also, in many respects, set them apart from their fellows.

Despite the fact that the majority of the boys had been Catholics, Bannow was still a boarding school, and the boys' surrogate parents had all been middle-class, hymn-signing, Protestant gentlemen, habituated by tradition into the philosophy of the stiff upper lip and respect for hierarchical class-based authority. In many respects, the boys had been the recipients of a very British education. Indeed, to the local Catholic farmers, secondary education would, in and of itself, have appeared a Protestant influence; a gift they could hardly refuse but which they suspected would cause their children to grow up despising their parents. For their children's sake, they suffered, rather than embraced, the greater opportunity.

In 1868, a correspondent to the *Dublin Evening Post*, having spent some time in Bannow as a visitor, and having interviewed several of the local farmers, found that bitterness still deeply entrenched forty-odd years after the closure of the school. Speculating on the 'true' causes of the failure of the school, those he interviewed opined that:

'These reasons were first that the agricultural teacher, a Scotchman, was more ignorant of his profession than were many of the fathers of the pupils, and, secondly, that the literary teacher was dreaded by the Catholics, who suspected him to be bent on aiding in "the new reformation" as it was so called.'

There is obviously a partisan element to these complaints that bears taking with a pinch of salt. Nevertheless, it betrays a locally held suspicion that, despite the religious education of the Catholic boys having been entrusted to the care of their parish priest, the pupils were being subjected to an unduly English and Protestant influence. It wasn't that long ago that the school's teachers could easily have found their heads on the end of a pike on foot of such allegations. They were, after all, peddling their influence in the county of Wexford less than a quarter of a century after the rebellion, and atrocities, of 1798.

Given the arena in which many of Bannow's better graduates would ultimately seek to find employment, a 'British' education was probably no bad thing. At the very least it prepared them for professional employment on the estates of the upper classes. For those who aspired to become land stewards, first impressions mattered, and first impressions had as much to do with bearing as blood.

At twenty years of age, William Kelly had big ambitions. He was not content to simply *be* a land steward. He wanted to be the best; a man like the famous authors whose books he had so admired at Bannow; perhaps even the Rev. William Hickey himself, who had published several works on agriculture and gained a modicum of literary fame under the pseudonym of 'Martin Doyle'.

Amongst Hickey's works are to be found such titles as *Hints to Small Farmers, Plea for Small Farmers, The Kitchen Garden, The Flower Garden*, and *The Agricultural Labourer Viewed*, titles and topics not a million miles away from those for which William Kelly himself would later become famous. Wherever Hickey had led, especially with regard to the aid and education of small farmers, or sympathy for the plight of the poor and downtrodden, William Kelly was destined not just to follow, but to surpass.

FARMHILL TO PORTRANE

WE LOSE SIGHT of William Kelly for several years after his graduation. During this time, according to his own testimony, his education continued in a self-directed manner. Many visits were made to successful farms in order to assess the effectiveness of their methods. Those he liked he adapted to his own ends; those he did not, he set his mind to improving.

A 'Mr Kelly', gardener to Mr James Ferrier of Willow Park in Booterstown, won several prizes for the cultivation of greenhouse plants such as grapes and peaches between 1827 and 1829 at the spring and summer exhibitions of the Royal Horticultural Society of Ireland. Ferrier served on the Dublin Chamber of Commerce with a certain Joseph Boyce (later Lord Mayor of Dublin), so it is at least possible that a personal connection to the Bannow Farm School existed.

If this *was* the same William Kelly, then it would suggest that he had found work in Dublin quite soon after leaving Bannow, but as a gardener rather than as a land agent or steward. It would have been steady work, and better paid than a farm labourer, but it would not have been what his apprenticeship had prepared him for.

All we know for certain is that, sometime about 1831, our William Kelly landed a job as land steward and gardener to Mr James Pratt of Farmhill, in south County Dublin. Pratt was the Deputy Sergeant at Arms for Ireland and his estate lay close to the village, as it was then, of Dundrum. He lived there with his wife, Julianna, and his three children. Pratt, coincidentally, was serving at that time on the Dublin Chamber of Commerce alongside James Ferrier.

The post of steward at Farmhill was several steps beyond the level of gardeners and ploughboys that so many other graduates of the Bannow Farm School had gone on to become. In his new role, Kelly would be called 'Mister' by his staff and ranked higher in the social pecking order than the family solicitor. Discovering that he had been given a cottage on the estate, he sent immediately for his mother.

In its entirety the Farmhill estate consisted of thirty-six acres and a newly built mansion of twenty-five rooms and two gate lodges. It wasn't large by Irish standards, but as Pratt's land steward, Kelly would be responsible for running the business of the estate, making it profitable, and keeping it in good order. He would need a head for figures, a talent for meticulous record-keeping and expertise in all aspects of agriculture, including the growing of peaches, of which James Pratt was extraordinarily fond, and of cherries, for which he would win a gold medal at the Irish Horticultural Society Exhibition at the Rotunda in June of 1835.

Kelly hated uncertainty and waste. Obsessed with efficiency, he possessed a deep-seated need for advance knowledge of *what* he would be doing and *when*. While working for the Pratts, he began to impose an almost mathematical order on the Farmhill estate and, in so doing, began to have the first stirrings of an idea. Collating, graphing, and organising his personal thoughts and practical experiences, he began, by degrees, to formulate something resembling a systematic method for the management of small to medium-sized estates.

This method, refined over several years, had proved itself robust at Farmhill, but it was essentially an adaptation of the work of others. If he was ever to see his name in print, he would need something that was uniquely his own. When he finally managed to feed eight head of cattle for an entire year on the produce of just two and a half acres of ground, he knew he had found it.

In just eighty pages, Kelly detailed his theories on the systematic management of what at the time were called 'villa farms', i.e. medium-sized estates of ten to twenty acres used primarily as the Dublin residences of wealthy judges, high ranking law officers, and professional or mercantile gentlemen. Such men, obliged to spend most of their time in the city, had little time to spend managing or improving their estates and became dependent upon the judgement of their stewards and gardeners. Unlike the graduates of the universities or agricultural colleges like Bannow, these men were not always the most educated or competent. The farms, in consequence, often became a burden to their owners.

He could help, Kelly believed, by educating these same stewards in the practical aspects of modern farm management. His system would be a simple process, easily understood and optimum in its use of resources. Employed correctly, it could help every one of these 'villa farms' to become an efficient and profitable concern:

'My object in referring to these topics is, to show that if the farmer gets his work done in a systematic manner, it will be done better, in every sense of the word – that it will come lighter on those who do it – and

that everything will be done in due time, and nothing left undone.

A man who superintends business in a gentleman's establishment must determine, every night, what work he is to have done on the following day; and not only this, but he must always have decided on the works that are to be done a month hence. He must always have a variety of works in view, to suit the season and different kinds of weather he may expect.

The men must be employed, not in a way by which to pass over time, but in such a way that there is work to be done equivalent to the money expended on having it done. Thus, then, he must first have an outline of the whole year's work; he can know from this what work is to be done in each quarter, and so on in each month, and down to each day – always regulating it, as nearly as possible, by the first plan determined on.'

Kelly published his system in 1836. The book was called *An essay on the general management of Villa Farms, the manures attainable, and applicable to such farms: also, a mode of cultivating two acres of ground, whereby eight cows can be fed throughout the year, with some remarks on the management of small farms in general.'* It was printed in Dublin by Joshua Porter, the printer who had previously published the reports of the Bannow Farm School.

In his book, Kelly offered a cost-benefit analysis of every aspect of farm management and detailed his proven systems of farm sub-division, crop rotation, manufacture of manure, and feeding of cattle. Many of his ideas were borrowed from Sir John Sinclair and Sir Humphry Davy, names he casually recited as though they had been his mentors. And in a way they had, for Sinclair's *Husbandry of Scotland* and Davy's *Elements of Agricultural Chemistry*, appear to have been required texts at the Bannow Farm School.

Kelly's publication, however, was much more than a handbook of agricultural management or an exploration of the application of scientific principles to the fertilisation of soil; it was an exercise in farm economics. Nothing of any value, from urine to waste food, could go to waste. The bottom line was always referenced.

Take, for example, his primary discovery on the feeding of cattle. Eight cows, he claimed, could be stall-fed from no more than two and a half acres. If they were to be pasture fed in the traditional manner, they would require more than three times that acreage:

'In order, therefore, to have plenty of hay, which, in every place, is a great object, it is requisite to have as much meadow as the farm will admit of; and, that there may be plenty of meadow, the cows should, as much as possible, be stall-fed. This is the key to the whole work for, without the stall-feeding, it is impossible to make plenty of manure; and without plenty of manure it is impossible to cultivate the farm to the advantage.'

Kelly also went so far as to recommend that Irish farmers reconsider the manner in which they grew potatoes, outlining the risks of low yields from poor winter management that he believed was rife across the country at that time. 'The season of planting,' he claimed, 'and the way the potatoes intended for seed are managed during the winter and previous to the time for planting, cause more failure than all the other evil agencies that are spoken of.' This was 1836. Nine years before the potato blight arrived in Ireland.

With regard to manure, there was a good deal of controversy and conflicting opinions in the world of agriculture at the time as to whether manure should be applied to the soil in a fresh or decomposed state. Kelly's conclusion was that for crops that would require immediate assistance from the manure, such as turnips and all annual crops, the more decomposed the dung the better the results. But when dung was to be ploughed into the soil or used for potatoes with the aim of improving the land for future crops, a moderate degree of decomposition was better. He also offered advice on such controversial subjects as the proper use of lime, soot, and salt.

Kelly went into great detail on the manufacture and application of manure, an analysis of which is beyond the scope of this book. What is important, to our purposes here, is merely to recognise in Kelly the traits of a born empiricist and the fact that the majority of his thoughts and 'experiments' were based on the study of organic chemistry, a science then very much in its infancy.

Apart from Davy and Sinclair, Kelly brandished such names as Brande, Fourcroy, and Vanquelin, like a swinging sword in defence of his methods. That he even knew of the ongoing work of such eminent scientists is indicative, at the very least, of the fact that his studies had not ceased upon his graduation.

Crucial to Kelly's 'system' was the division of the Villa Farm into functional units. On a farm of 20 acres, for example, he suggested the following:

Division	Acres
4 field of 2.5 acres each	10.0
Garden	1.0
Shrubberies & Ornamental Planting	1.5
Hay Yard, Dung Yard etc.	0.5
Lawn, House, Office, Yard & Avenues	7.0
Total	20.0

From this Kelly created a further grid for the four fields and a personalised system of crop rotation which involved the green crops moving to a new field every five years:

Year	Field 1	Field 2	Field 3	Field 4
1	Potatoes	Oats	Wheat	Green Crops
2	Wheat	Potatoes	Oats	"
3	Oats	Wheat	Potatoes	"
4	Potatoes	Oats	Wheat	"
5	2.0 Wheat 0.5 Oats & Clover	Potatoes	Oats	"
6	Green Crops	Wheat	Potatoes	Oats

There was much that was admirable and modern in Kelly's book, but it never really took off and copies of it to this day are difficult to find. Nevertheless, it must have been of some specialised horticultural interest, because twenty-seven years later he would still be referring to himself in his letters to the press as the author of *this* work rather than a subsequent publication that had attracted far greater public attention and acclaim.

At this stage of his young life, William Kelly is beginning to show signs of empirical thinking, but he is still very much influenced by the education he received at Bannow. He borrows heavily from his old textbooks, and even from his old mentor, the Rev. William Hickey. Kelly's section on the work of the Rev. Richard Radcliffe of Enniscorthy, in fact, is heavily influenced by *Hints for the Small Farmers of Ireland,* a work written six years previous by Hickey under the pseudonym of 'Martin Doyle'.

But it has ever been such. Imitation is the necessary precursor to singularity and Kelly's efforts represented more than opportunistic palimpsests or plagiarism, they included improvements and refinements born of practical and specific experience. Many of the ideas and recommendations that Kelly espoused in this book would, inevitably, be further altered, improved, or discarded, by the time he next published. But for now, having tried on his master's coat and found that it fitted him uncommonly well, his first published work filled him with renewed purpose and self-confidence.

He had done well for himself. He had proven himself a talented farmer and had climbed the social ladder to a rank of respectability. Secure in his employment and already a published author, he had a fine cottage in which to live and prospects for the future. And yet, even still, he had higher ambitions. His first book represented more than a record of his systems and experiments, it represented a surreptitiously placed calling card, a demonstration of his credentials.

William Kelly celebrated his thirtieth birthday, and his mother her seventy-fifth, in the year he made the first truly momentous decision of his life. At this age, the obstacle of maternal approval would have been a low hurdle for any prospective bride to clear, but Elizabeth Kelly could never have anticipated her son's choice of a wife.

On Saturday, 17 September 1836, William Kelly donned his Sunday best and presented himself at St. Mary's Pro Cathedral in Dublin where he was solemnly joined in holy wedlock to one Mary Jane Shanks, a mature woman nine years his senior. Given the age difference, it is unlikely they had engaged the services of a matchmaker. The witnesses were Robert Pooler, assistant secretary of the Royal Horticultural Society of Ireland – indicative of the circles in which Kelly was now moving – and a certain Margaret Crawford.

A mature woman might have intimidated a lesser man; made him fearful of veiled allusions and private ridicule. It wasn't as if he was marrying into money. Indeed, the opposite, would appear to have been the case. Mary Jane's brother, James Shanks, lived at 65 Lower Mecklenburg Street, right in the heart of Dublin's tenement district and, if her brother's address was anything to go by, Mary Jane, too, would have been a poor, working-class woman.

At thirty-nine, Mary Jane Shanks knew a little more about the world than her new husband. She had known the ridicule of spinsterhood and the shame of being a burden on her family. Her expectations, in consequence, would have been realistic – no small matter, given the life she was heading into.

She had made a good match – she would have known that – had married a highly moral man; a man who would be good to her; a man from a 'respectable' profession who, despite his fine clothes and expanding girth, could never forget his roots. In every sense of the word, William Kelly was the perfectly right gentleman for Mary Jane Shanks. The obverse? Well, that remained to be seen.

Nineteenth-century women were expected to marry and to have children, and men were expected to marry women who would bear them sons who would carry on the family name. For Mary Jane, that obligation would now be a race against both time and nature. At thirty-nine she was, by the standards of the day, at an advanced age for conception. William's mother had given birth to him at forty-five, it was true, but there could be no guarantees. They would both have been well aware of that as they lay that first night on their marriage bed.

That having been said, neither of them would ever have to endure the ritual humiliation of 'Chalk Sunday' again; to run the cruel gauntlet of teenage boys who would loiter outside the church on the first Sunday in Lent, waiting to place the mark of shame upon the unmarried. It was a tradition as old as the hills, but it was also a form of bullying, of attaching guilt to a matter that was not really anyone else's business and largely out of their control. Marriage had bought them respectability. They could at least be thankful for that.

Chalk Sunday © Illustrated London News Ltd/Mary Evans

Four years flew by. They endured the cold and dismal summer of '37 and the subsequent failure of the potato crop. They witnessed famine and poverty and the introduction of the Poor Law and came through largely unscathed. And they saw the youthful and pink-cheeked Victoria, already being romanticised as 'England's Rose', ascend the British throne, heralding an era of optimism, progress, and moral rebirth.

They had been blessed in so many ways, but perhaps not in the manner they most desired, for Mary Jane's biological clock never chimed. And so they kept themselves busy, scorning all excuses for complacency. If a young girl could rule an empire, then who was to say that any lesser ambition was impossible.

After four years at Farmhill, Mary Jane would by now have become well acquainted with the challenges and duties of being a steward's wife. She would have come to know her husband's strengths and weaknesses, where and when to be familiar with his workers, and how to organise the feeding of them at harvest. She had, in many respects, served her own apprenticeship. They were ready for a bigger challenge.

The opportunity, when it arrived, came from a plain-spoken woman considered something of an oddity in Dublin social circles. She lived on the far side of the county on an isolated peninsula more renowned for pirates, smuggling, and shipwrecks than for agriculture. Her name was Sophia Evans, only daughter of the late Sir John Parnell, former Chancellor of the Exchequer of Ireland and Lord of the Treasury. Two of her brothers had been MPs and her husband, George, was currently the member for Dublin.

If there was anyone in the county likely to have read William Kelly's book on villa farms, it was Sophia Evans, a largely self-educated agnostic with a keen interest in politics, philosophy, and the natural sciences. As a member of the Irish Horticultural Society, she had even presided as a judge at some of the exhibitions at which William Kelly had previously competed.

Whatever references or recommendations had been made on his behalf, they must have been powerful, for despite his lack of experience in managing estates of this size, Sophia Evans, sometime about the year 1838, hired William Kelly to modernise her husband's estate. We need to exercise some historical imagination here to understand the scale of this achievement, and what it would have meant for a non-university educated Catholic to have taken on so large an estate just four years after the granting of Catholic Emancipation. This was no simple head-gardener position.

The Evans estate offered an opportunity for Kelly to test his methods on an industrial scale. From a villa farm of just thirty-six acres, he was now expected to take charge of an estate over *sixty* times that size. Not having managed anything quite so grand before, it was a daunting prospect that required, not just an advanced level of skill and education, but an unshakeable belief in one's own ability.

As the steward of an estate the size of Portrane, William could now expect to earn anything from £100 to £300 a year. In return, he would be expected to supervise a veritable army of gardeners, labourers, grooms, coachmen, herdsmen, gamekeepers, yardmen, blacksmiths, foresters, carpenters, and stonemasons. Some knowledge of law would also be required if he was to successfully manage contracts and leases, something he would have had little experience of at Farmhill. If successful, and if he managed his money carefully, he would soon be a moderately wealthy young man.

It mattered now, more than ever, that he had married a fully functioning adult who could cope with the challenges that lay ahead; who could take on the new cottage and servants and, with a kindly but unbending manner, make the place her own. His wife would be his eyes and ears about a village where petty resentments were to be expected amongst those whose rents he collected, and also about the estate, where it was almost inevitable that workers would be tempted to see her as a shortcut to his favour.

There would also, inevitably, be some who would see in the fact that the Kellys were a Catholic couple who shared a weekly communion with them, the right to be overly familiar. In dealing with all of these, and more, Mary Jane would require a diplomatic tongue and a sympathetic ear. She could not afford to make her husband's job impossible.

And then there was the small matter of age. Her looks would fade, quicker than his no doubt, and there would be the usual whispers, amusement, and prejudicial assumptions. All of that was a given, a part of the bargain they had made with God. The estate would be one challenge, the parish quite another. Sunday masses would be a minefield of potential missteps.

The Kellys had barely settled into their new cottage at Middlefield when disaster hit. On the night of 5 January 1839, Ireland suffered a heavy snowfall, perhaps a little less heavy in Donabate and Portrane because of its proximity to the sea than in nearby Swords, but enough to occupy the children the following morning while their parents prepared for the festivities of the Epiphany.

Sometime in the middle of the afternoon, the clouds stopped moving and the sun struggled to break through the thick cover. The air became so eerily still that people could hear the voices of neighbours living over a mile away.

Ever so slowly, the air began to heat and the snow to melt. A deep depression in the Atlantic began to push a warm front eastwards over the country. Temperatures rose by ten degrees and people began to complain of an unseasonable and 'sickly' humidity. As the warm front rose in the atmosphere, it was replaced, sometime about dusk, by a cold front that brought a slight breeze and light rain that gradually turned to heavy rain and hail.

By midnight the winds were roaring at 185km an hour – hurricane force 12 on the Beaufort Scale or Category 3 on the Saffir–Simpson. Ireland had never experienced anything like it. It was a storm equivalent to the famous Hurricane Katrina that devasted the U.S. states of Florida and Louisiana in August 2005.

At about 3 a.m. the wind shifted direction, bringing

with it rain and hail 'driven with such violence as, in some instances, to break the glass of windows.' The wind remained at that force until about five o'clock the following morning, creating chaos, terror, and pitch darkness across the whole of north County Dublin.

In some places, a red aurora could be seen in the northern sky; in others, the only light to be had came from lightning strikes. Trees came down, walls and houses collapsed, rivers burst their banks, and roofs and livestock were blown away. Fires were even started by embers that had been whipped into the sky and fallen on something flammable, like hay or thatch.

By the time daylight came and the dazed and exhausted population, who hadn't dared to sleep, began to slowly creep from their positions of shelter, the old Dutch windmill at Feltrim had lost its great sails, and the Anglican church at Lusk had lost its roof and quarter of the houses in north County Dublin had been destroyed. Thousands of families were left homeless; more in a single night than in the decade of evictions that would follow the famine. The greater Fingal area, with tens of thousands of fallen trees, resembled the type of wasteland one generally associated with the aftermath of a great artillery battle.

Hardest hit, other than those who had died or lost loved ones in the storm, were the small tenant farmers who had lost their homes and had their savings scattered on the wind (it had been common practice to hide money in the thatch). Corn and hay, whipped from the haggards by the hurricane, had been strewn across the waterlogged fields, leaving them with no means of feeding their surviving livestock through what remained of the winter. Roads, rivers, and trenches were blocked, and flooding was widespread. Dead birds lay everywhere. For months afterwards, the dawn chorus was silent, the evening sky bereft of the croak of ravens.

For William and Mary Jane, though roof damage would have been inevitable, their cottage had been left standing. They had survived, which was more than could be said for the estate that William had been hired to manage. There would be no flowers grown for fêtes or horticultural exhibitions that year, or indeed the next. There were other, more immediate priorities. On the positive side, the crisis afforded him an opportunity to prove his mettle.

Two years after the 'night of the big wind', William found himself caught up in a public enquiry. It took place on 30 July of that year and concerned the competence of a certain Mr Taylor, a surveyor who had previously worked for the Balrothery Poor Law Union.

Taylor had left Balrothery under something of a cloud. Invited by Kelly to value the Evans estate Taylor had never actually visited the demesne. According to Kelly's landlord, George Evans, he had made his wildly inaccurate valuation at Waters' Public House in Swords.

Taylor's valuation had over-estimated the Portrane Demesne by some sixty-four acres, and the entire parish of Portrane by almost twice that. Having brought the discrepancy to the attention of his landlord, Kelly was sent back to Taylor armed with ordnance survey maps. Taylor refused to amend his figures, at least in front of Kelly, but he later amended them in private. The enquiry, on the other hand, was anything but private. It was splashed all over the pages of the *Leinster Express*.

Apart from that, the first of his many appearances in the column inches of Irish newspapers, William Kelly kept a low profile, working assiduously and innovatively at turning the Evans estate into a modern and profitable agricultural concern. At the same time, he continued to record and measure everything he attempted with scientific accuracy, ready to share his findings with the world at large should he happen upon another noteworthy discovery. In Kelly's mind, agriculture was a science and, to be successful at it in an era of scientific and industrial revolution, farming also needed to be scientific.

As the steward of an estate of the size of Portrane, William Kelly now had a responsibility to both the estate and to the wider community that depended upon it. He employed the head gardener, head gamekeeper and paid the wages of their workmen. Touring the estate on horseback, he also collected rents, supervised the tenantry, and settled squabbles. The people skills that permitted William Kelly to not only succeed at Portrane but to garner universal respect, would be the very same skills that would make him such an effective and trustworthy political activist in later life.

William Kelly would never be a great public speaker, and his accent would always mask his education and betray his origins. His ability to organise, to see the bigger picture, to plan ahead and achieve consensus, however, these were the mark of a persuader, of the type of man that gets things done and holds any enterprise, be it political or agricultural, together. Garrulous and loquacious at times, he had a wry and grim sense of humour that occasionally bordered on self-parody. But, behind the bucolic charm, there was always a degree of humility and self-deprecation that made people want to listen to him. For all his skills as an agriculturalist, his greatest talent, perhaps, lay in his ability to manage people.

Spreading his knowledge and know-how amongst the estate's tenant farmers, Kelly worked hand-in-glove with the landlord's wife, Mrs Sophia Evans, who had pretty much taken over the modernisation of the estate while her husband, George, concentrated on his legal career in Dublin. Sophia had already begun to re-design the grounds according to her personal preferences when Kelly arrived, but she had always been open to new ideas, especially those with a proven basis in science.

The success of the land reclamation efforts at Bannow would have been well known to George and Sophia Evans as reports on the project had been ordered and compiled for the British House of Commons, where George Evans sat as the member for Dublin. And now that the storm damage had been cleared and repaired, there was a reclamation job waiting to be completed. The acreage of the Evans' estate was not reflected in its income, and Sophia wanted Kelly, with his modern approach and Bannow experience, to remedy that. It was a challenge he accepted with relish.

George Hampden Evans' election to the House of Commons in 1834, obliged his wife to travel with him each year for the 'London Season'. Possessed of big ideas, but with diminishing time to dedicate to the estate, she needed a modern steward whose ambition matched her own; a man she could trust. She did not need a steward who required 'handling'.

Sophia had moved in feminist circles in Paris where she had known Madame de Stäel; had been a friend of Margaret King before her days as a transvestite medical student and mentor to Percy and Mary Shelley. She had also been an intimate of the influential Condorcet family and had carried private correspondence to Elizabeth Patterson Bonaparte in Paris. She may even have met the Empress Josephine. Indeed, so many of her early influences had been French, it was a wonder the family coat-of-arms had not been replaced by a *fleur-de-lys*.

Described variously as *une maitress femme* and a resolute character with the 'face of a lioness', Sophia Evans was no soft touch. This largely self-educated intellectual, who had recently become friendly with the family of Charles Darwin, had long nurtured an interest in the natural sciences and was in the process of collating an extensive collection of Irish seashells. In her younger years, she had come under the influence of the agriculturalist, Arthur Young, whom she had met in Paris, and had long desired a steward of similar calibre to help her convert estate into a profitable business. She could not, however, supervise every detail in person. She was a society lady whose husband had a career. Her place was by his side, wherever he might be.

Come March of each year, just as the farm became a hive of vernal activity, the big house would be closed, the furniture covered with dust sheets, and wardrobes transferred to leather and wooden trunks. The Evans family would swap evening strolls along the cliffs at Tower Bay for high society boating trips on the Thames. Until the end of July each year, they would entrust the running of their vast estate to William Kelly. They would pray that the harvest would be good and that on their return they would find everything as they had left it, or much improved. If they did not, there would be hell to pay.

Kelly, too, had read Young, and in later years would quote him at length in his letters to the press. Like Young, Kelly, too, was capable of rhapsodising on the subjects of manure and the need for agricultural modernization, though his sympathy for, and understanding of, the countryside economy was far more empathetic than Young's for having been raised in a community of smallholders reduced to wage labour by modernization.

Like Young, Kelly saw himself, not as a common 'salt of the earth' farmer or rustic savant, but as an agricultural scientist, a potential educator, a man who could help to modernise the farming practices of a backward nation and make a reputation for himself in the process. To realise his ambition, he needed an employer liberal, wealthy, and willing enough to grant him the land, and indeed the time, to complete his experiments. In Sophia Evans, it appeared, he had found one.

BLIGHT

PRIOR TO THE start of the industrial revolution, Ireland had traditionally been a grazing economy, but rising demand from the expanding industrial cities in Britain increased the demand for grains such as oats and barley. With the growth of Dublin's breweries and rising prices in England, landlords raced to reclaim waste land to grow grains. This required increasingly greater numbers of farm labourers, whose numbers grew so swiftly that they soon accounted for half the population of Leinster.

These field labourers, the dregs of the social scale, were largely dependent on casual employment. Those lucky enough to find regular work would often be given a small cottage by their landlords and about an acre of land. By 1845 the number of these single-acre 'farms' amounted to 135,000. On these tiny plots, a man would be expected to grow everything he needed to feed his family.

For the most part, these labourers referred to themselves as 'small' farmers. To their own ears, it sounded less plebeian. In north County Dublin, the vast majority of them congregated on commonage around the village of Swords.

Approximately three-quarters of the Irish population depended on farming for their livelihood and many of the poorest lived in one-room mud cabins with little more than straw beds, rudimentary tables, wooden stools, and an iron pot. Their homes were frequently damp, even in summer and, apart from the farmer and his family, their farms would often have to grow sufficient food to support a horse, a cow, some chickens, and a pig.

But no matter how much, or how little, land the poor man leased, his methods of crop rotation remained simple and primitive. When the wheat was harvested potatoes were sown, and vice versa, each crop preparing the soil for the other. The potatoes would be harvested to feed his family, and the more expensive grain crops sold to pay the rent, to feed the horse, and to buy clothes. By 1800 the potato had become the staple of his diet.

But it hadn't always been so.

Back in 1740, famine had killed between 300,000 and 500,000 people – a much higher percentage of the population at that time than would be affected by the famine of 1845. This earlier famine had been triggered by a sequence of poor weather that had reduced grain harvests, frost damaged the potatoes, and led to a shortage of milk.

At that time oats, rather than potatoes, were the staple of the poor. In fact, as late as 1836, the diet of farm labourers on the Portrane peninsula was still being documented as consisting mainly of wheaten bread (cooked on a griddle), oatmeal porridge, potatoes, and buttermilk.

By 1845, however, the population of the country had tripled, grain prices had rocketed, and the average income was now half of what it was in the rest of the United Kingdom. Oats and wheat, furthermore, were now beyond the purses of the poorest as a regular source of nutrition.

The cheap and nutritious potato, on the other hand, offered the considerable advantage of not having to be processed, thus saving the farmer the cost of milling. The poorest third of the population could now *only* afford the potato and, in the west and south of the country, were increasingly sowing a single variety, the Lumper, which had been introduced to Ireland from Scotland in the 1800s.

The Lumper had proved to be a sturdy and reliable potato that required little manure, thrived in poor soil, and provided greater yields than most other varieties. Indeed, a single acre could produce over two thousand pounds of potatoes, enough to feed a family of four. But the Lumper was pretty much tasteless and favoured only by those who could not afford to buy anything else.

Varieties such as the Apple and the Cup were preferred by those who could afford to grow them, and most especially by William Kelly, who cultivated them at Portrane alongside less popular varieties such as the Bangor and the Pink-Eye. All along the east coast, from Skerries to Wexford, the Lumper was hardly sown at all, nor, indeed, was it in Ulster. The multiple varieties that *were* sown, however, would prove to be no more resistant to blight than the much-maligned Lumper.

By 1845 the potato accounted for a third of Irish agricultural output, but monoculture on this scale was always going to be a risky strategy. Should the crop fail, there would be no cheaper food available to switch to. When the blight arrived in Europe, countries like Belgium, Holland, and Denmark were also affected, but in no other European country did the population depend so much on a single root crop. It was a catastrophe waiting to happen.

Prior to the arrival of the blight, the small farmers of Ireland rarely suffered from extreme privation. As long as the peasant farmer had 'his supper in the ridge', he was, as William Kelly would later write, 'quite independent of care, comparatively so of energy and, generally speaking, of industry'.

A Blighted Potato

This summation might on first reading appear harsh, but it held sufficient truth for the upper classes to find in the potato dependence of the Irish poor, the stencil of a racial stereotype. The Irish were a 'lazy' people, dependent by choice upon a 'lazy root' that they grew in 'lazy' beds; a root that produced such an abundance of food for so little effort that it fostered 'from the earliest childhood, habits of indolence, improvidence and waste.'

This was, of course, an oversimplification. The

small farmer *did* grow other crops. Those who could, would grow a small number of green crops and raise pigs on scraps to be eaten or sold in the summer. For those lucky enough to live near a large city, surplus potatoes could also be sold rather than left to rot.

Whatever money the small farmer might get for his pig, if not also used to pay the rent, generally went on clothing for the family. Eggs, fowl, and everything else that could generate a surplus, he sold to buy tea, tobacco, and other 'necessities', but rarely food. For *that* he generally relied solely on the potato, consuming as many as forty-five per day. It made sound economic and nutritional sense, so long as the crop never failed.

When added to milk, the potato was something of a wonder food. It provided more than enough protein, carbohydrates, energy, and minerals, for a balanced and healthy diet. But there was a snag. Potatoes could not be stored for longer than nine months, and so, for three months every summer, there would be no potatoes at all. Farm labourers who took to the roads in search of work each spring would often leave their families to beg for food during the 'hungry months' of June and July before the new crop of potatoes was harvested.

Few, it seemed, cared enough to invest their time and energy into finding a practical solution. But William Kelly did. He had left Bannow a modest and highly moral young man sensitive to the ignorance and vulnerability of those neighbours that were locked into the inertia of extreme poverty and had already applied his systems to the management of medium-sized farms. Scaling his methods down to a single acre would surely be no great task.

But farms, like the men and women who worked them, were not mathematical equations, they were extremely complex organisms. If his solutions were to convince, he needed data, or, as Sinclair would put it, statistics. Kelly would not publish what he had not first tried and tested at Portrane.

In his partnership with Sophia Evans, William Kelly had begun almost immediately upon his employment to re-organise the Evans estate and to advise its tenant farmers on modern and scientifically proven practices. Just as he had seen done at Bannow, his first act had been to set about reclaiming a vast amount of marshy land in order to broaden the range of produce that could be grown locally. This had had the dual consequence of increasing his employer's arable acreage and providing steady, non-seasonal employment for local labourers.

In 1841, Kelly burned the surface of eight acres of marshy ground and then, fertilizing it with just the ashes, sowed turnips, potatoes, and mangelwurzel in order to break up the ground for the later cultivation of wheat. He also began to experiment with cultivation and crop rotation, his experiments proving so successful that his agricultural produce was soon winning prizes for his employer at the Royal Dublin Society.

The following year, in the wake of the sudden death of her husband, Sophia Evans began to take a more hands-on interest in the running of her estates. She was determined to prove that a woman could be an effective landlord, and determined to take her rightful place on the prize winners' rostrums of the RDS agricultural shows alongside the great landowners of the plains of Meath and Kildare.

Encouraged by Kelly's recent successes, she began to invest in his studies and to allow him greater time and land upon which to experiment. Kelly, in return, continued to increase her stock of arable land through reclamation and draining. It was a partnership unequal in all manners, except that of respect.

As it had been at Bannow, the digging of irrigation ditches was back-breaking work, though not without the occasional surprise. One glorious June day in 1843, while digging an irrigation ditch in Portrane,

Kelly's midge-tormented labourers uncovered the remains of a *megaloceros giganteus*. The head and antlers of the prehistoric creature were in such a perfect state of preservation that no one who saw them could fail to imagine the size of the living elk.

For a while, the eight-foot span of the seven-thousand-year-old antlers became a subject of both local and national curiosity. Many believed it to be the remains of a creature that had drowned in the biblical flood: too large to fit aboard the ark. Had they known what was coming, this ancient curiosity might have appeared to the watchers of signs and portents as an omen: a lesson that when it came to natural disasters, as they had learnt to their cost in 1839, God had his favourites.

In 1845, Sophia Evans gave Kelly an entire field in which to experiment with different strains of wheat. She agreed to take a loss on the field, having been convinced by Kelly to look upon it as a long-term investment. Thirty-one different varieties were sown in parallel drills twenty-one inches apart, with half a pound of seed to every ten perches of drill. Bad weather compromised the study and the following summer only five perches of each variety were weighed. The results, nevertheless, would be considered of such scientific importance as to be published in both the *Irish Farmers' Journal* in Dublin and *The Farmers' Magazine* in London.

The bringing in of the wheat harvest each August was usually a cause for celebration in country villages. In Portrane, this usually took place in a field that was once located behind where The Brook public house currently stands but has long since been reclaimed by the sea. The celebration, called 'Pattern Sunday' consisted of traditional singing and dancing, wrestling and football, and the occasional faction fight with the residents of Donabate.

Traditionally, people would visit nearby St. Cudget's

well, to place offerings, recite the rosary and drink the water, which was alleged to contain miraculous and curative properties. The festival was the biggest event of the year in the parish, and a source of such merriment and celebration as would lift the mood of the inhabitants for weeks afterwards. But not that year.

Just two weeks after the Pattern celebrations of 1845, the potato crop was struck by blight. At its outset, it accounted for 75% of the potato crop in the Fingal area and between 33% and 50% nationally. It would have been only too easy to allow oneself to be paralysed by pessimism in the face of such odds, but in Portrane, Kelly, quick to recognise the implications, chose to turn the crisis on its head and see in the increasing numbers of unemployed, an opportunity for mutual assistance.

Moving swiftly, Kelly stabled his farming machinery and began to engage as many people as he could in manual labour, primarily in irrigation and reclamation work. Even the children of the poor found occasional work in the sowing of seeds. The work he generated, provided an income for many families whose potatoes had been lost and who would otherwise have been unable to buy food.

The Fingal area, in general, managed to get through that year without any great upheaval and the land was cropped again in much the same way. The following year, when the crop failed again, the first deaths from starvation began to be recorded, or at least they did outside of the Portrane peninsula.

The initial response of the Tory government had been generous but, in June 1846, they were replaced by a Whig government led by Lord John Russell who had been elected on a platform of minimal state intervention and a conviction that it was the responsibility of local landlords and charities, and not of the government, to save the starving masses. Irish resources were to be used to solve what was deemed to be an Irish rather than a British problem. Some landlords would be bankrupted by the cost, others would steadfastly refuse to contribute.

In September 1846, a delegation of ninety-five labourers from Swords petitioned Charles Cobbe of Newbridge House for relief work, which he forwarded to the government. It led to the formation of a local relief committee. By October, four of the country's one hundred and thirty workhouses were already full. Three months later workhouses nationally held nearly one hundred thousand people, the local workhouse at Balrothery was full, and 3,000 local people in the area of Swords and its environs were said to be in 'extreme' want.

If she had ever doubted the wisdom of marrying a man nine years her junior, Mary Jane Kelly counted her blessings now. She was fortunate to be living in a fine cottage so close to the sea. She had fresh air and bracing walks on her doorstep, servants to help run the household, and a variety of fresh food in the pantry.

For her family in the city, however, and for the labouring classes of greater Fingal, life was infinitely more challenging. Swords, for example, had by now become the agricultural labour centre for half of north Dublin. The town was surrounded by a considerable amount of commonage on which farm labourers had built houses and enclosed gardens. When the potato crop failed the majority of these labourers struggled, not only to find work, but to afford an alternative source of food.

In response to the widespread hardship, Kelly decided to share with the farming public the economics behind his decision to forego the use of machines and utilise the local children to sow his fields by means of the dibble, a decision that was beginning to look not just fortuitous, but clairvoyant. A paper he wrote of the subject was widely read and his methods began, to a miniscule degree in the grand scheme of things, to be copied.

The Farmer's Gazette quoted one such farmer on 3 October 1846:

'Dibbling is expensive certainly; but if you save as much seed as will more than pay the expense, as you will perceive on reading the report of Mr William Kelly ... what can be better than to employ the poor, starving, helpless children of your neighbourhood at such useful works? We hope you will do so. We mean to do so ourselves this season.'

But of course, it wasn't only the *children* of the poor families of Portrane and Donabate that Kelly was providing employment for, he also took advantage of increasing local unemployment to provide work for their parents as well. That November, when asked what the most important and profitable works the farm labourers of Ireland could be presently employed at, Kelly responded:

'This is a question which has engaged the attention of the wisest and best men in the empire, and if we may judge from the various public works in progress throughout the country – the solution seems difficult. Now if I can look at the question in its true state, I really think the solution is quite easy, and consists in the two following short sentences, viz. – Drain all the ground that requires it; and trench, or subsoil all the ground on which you intend to grow green crops next season. These are, in my humble opinion, the only works at which the extra labour of the country should be engaged at present.

We may have hunger – we may have famine this year, and we cannot perhaps avert them; but we can take means to prevent a recurrence of them next year, simply, by cultivating green crops – and by what is an indispensable preliminary step to their successful cultivation, viz. draining and trenching, we can alleviate the wants and sufferings of the poor man during the present and coming season, by giving him employment, and consequently means to purchase food.

Well, then, I submit, that the people should be employed draining and trenching the ground, and that this ground, being drained and trenched, shall be cropped next year with turnips, mangel, carrots, parsnips, cabbages and vetches – the latter to be used for soiling cattle – and these green crops will, I maintain, be in some shape or other, the cheapest and the easiest procured substitute for the potato next year.

We are told to break up more ground – to sow a greater quantity of wheat and oats than usual, and also rye and bere. Of this recommendation I cannot approve. It might be the means of giving us plenty of food next year, providing it, the produce, were left in the country to be consumed by the people; but it would be the cause of such destruction to the land that we might be certain of short crops, and consequently short commons, for many years afterwards; whereas, by cultivating the turnips and the carrot &c., a sufficiency of food will be procured with more certainty, and the ground, instead of being deteriorated will be very much improved.

There is no doubt but that there will be more wheat and oats sown in Ireland this year than there should be – much of it on land not capable of growing half a crop of either – and the graziers, who have land, that if broken up would produce good crops, will hesitate long before they do break them up for that purpose. My advice is to sow only the same quantity of wheat and oats as usual, to sow an equal part, as of wheat or oats with peas and beans, and another equal part with turnips, &c., &c., and also an equal part with clover and Italian rye-grass.

Heretofore the small farmer paid his rent, &c., almost exclusively by the sale of his wheat and oats. Now I wish him to be able to meet these engagements by the sale of a few beasts, and have his grain cops, parsnips, cabbages, &c., for his own and family's use – but to accomplish this desirable object, the ground for the turnips and other roots, should be first drained, if wet, and then trenched – that is, a fourth or fifth of the land under cultivation should be treated so this present winter. See the amount of employment this would give. If we take the arable land of Ireland at 17,500,000 acres, and suppose the fifth of this was drained and trenched, why the trenching alone would employ one million of men for nearly six months, allowing 50 men to trench an acre – and this is at work that should be done, even if there was no particular object in employing the people at present.'

There, in a nutshell, was the means by which disaster could have been averted. The only problem – and it was a big one – was that it was not in the gift of the land agents and tenant farmers to implement it. That power lay entirely in the gift of the landlords, who were being asked to invest in a project that would, at least initially, incur a loss. Fearful of bankruptcy, few were prepared to listen; hardly surprising given that so many of them were absentee landlords.

After centuries of ruthless exploitation of their Irish estates by the Anglo-Irish Ascendancy, the new Whig government, in the mistaken belief that Irish landlords would not allow their own people to starve, decided to hold back on providing state aid or interfering in the grain market in the misguided expectation that it would force Irish landowners to take responsibility for the consequences of their greed. Some did, and it cost them dearly. Very many did not.

In Sophia Evans, however, Kelly enjoyed the confidence of a generous and liberal-minded patron. He had asked her to invest in his schemes before, and it had paid off handsomely. She was not about to desert her tenants or her neighbours, but neither was she about to risk bankruptcy by providing meaningless relief work. Kelly's reversion to manual labour, therefore, proved timely and opportune. During the ravages of the coming winter and the food shortages of the following year, Sophia Evans' tenants would be spared, while the country at large would be devastated.

THE DONABATE CHARTISTS

THE FAILURE OF the potato crop heralded great hardship for the tenant farmers of the Portrane peninsula but, for some, it represented something of a political opportunity. Patrick Ryan, the Parish Priest of Donabate, had been converted to Chartism while working as a priest amongst the Catholic miners and linen workers of Bradford and Barnsley in West Yorkshire. On his return to Ireland, he had established a small Chartist organisation in Donabate and joined it to the national body, the freshly formed Irish Universal Suffrage Association.

The membership of the IUSA consisted mainly of artisans, tradesmen, and £40 freeholders who had lost the vote in 1829. Their president, Patrick O'Higgins, was a wool merchant. Only in Donabate was the membership dominated by small farmers and farm labourers. That was entirely down to the charismatic leadership of the Rev. Patrick Ryan.

The Chartists were a parliamentary reform movement that had been founded in 1837 according to the principles of a manifesto called *The People's Charter*. It called for universal suffrage for men, equal electoral districts, voting by secret ballot, abolition of property qualifications for MPs, and annual general elections. Their primary strategy was to use petitions and mass gatherings to put pressure on politicians and their methods were largely peaceful and constitutional, apart from occasional insurrectionary outbreaks, most notably in South Wales and in

Yorkshire.

In 1839 and 1842, the Chartists managed to present petitions signed by millions of working people to the British House of Commons. That level of support, however, was never replicated in Ireland, where the movement was opposed by Daniel O'Connell. His 'Repeal' movement, of which William Kelly was an ardent supporter, was the dominant political force amongst Catholics in Ireland and intolerant of any other movement that might dilute or weaken it. In October 1841, in response to an allegation by O'Connell that the Chartists were essentially an English organisation dominated by Orangemen and Tories, the Catholic Chartists of Barnsley wrote an open letter of appreciation to Father Ryan in Donabate, to:

'... remove the unfavourable impression which such imputations are calculated to make upon the minds of our unhappy brethren in Ireland'.

Ryan attempted to get this letter, signed by over one hundred of the most prominent Catholic members of the movement in England,[1] printed in the *Freeman's Journal*, but was refused on the grounds that it was effectively an advertisement and would have to be paid for as such. The letter was subsequently printed in the pages of the *Northern Star*, a north of England newspaper that was effectively a Chartist periodical.

Father Ryan was very much the driving force behind the Chartist organization in Donabate and the *bête noire,* not just of the local Repeal Association, but of his archbishop. In choosing to join the Chartist movement Ryan had broken ranks from the official church position and caused a bit of a stir. The majority of the Catholic hierarchy were hostile to Chartism, and Chartists had frequently been denounced from the

[1] Burland, John Hugh. MS Annals of Barnsley, pp 186-188.

altar. Some priests even tried to intimidate Chartists by refusing to baptise their children and withholding the sacraments until they had withdrawn from the Association and surrendered their membership cards to them.

The enmity between the two movements was extreme. The Leicester Chartists dubbed O'Connell 'one of the vilest traitors and political apostates recorded in the annals of delinquency'. The Halifax Chartists declared him to be 'Satan amongst the Angels of Heaven' and the Chartists of Hull organized public burnings of his portrait. O'Connell and his supporters were no less scathing. They labelled the Chartists variously as 'wretched', 'miscreants', 'violent and unthinking', 'the worst enemies of Ireland', and 'evil'.

Ryan, like the Chartists themselves, was at his most politically potent between 1841 and 1844, when he became active in the organisation of petitions. The first of these, drafted in 1842, was titled *Chartism and Repeal* and argued for an alliance between Irish Repealers and English Chartists. The second, in 1843, was called *Civil and Religious Liberty* and dealt with the persecution of Irish Chartists by Daniel O'Connell and the Irish Clergy. Very much a maverick within his own church, Ryan quickly managed to split his community.

In Donabate, there were now two opposing Catholic factions – the Repeal Association and the Chartists – who actually supported many of the same causes, *including* Repeal. How many people had joined the IUSA in Donabate is difficult to assess. It is unlikely to have been large, but, at the same time, it was obviously significant enough a number for the population to consider calling for extra police when the enmity between the two groups became heated.

A measure of that enmity can perhaps be gleaned from a letter written by the Rev. Patrick Ryan to the *Freeman's Journal* shortly before he decided to join the

IUSA in 1841:

'It is melancholy to observe the diabolical spirit of ill-will and hatred which, has been recently infused into the minds of some ignorant persons in this city. I have, I regret to say, experienced this personally.

A man, whose name I shall now forbear to mention, but who is the same person to whom the "Loyal National Repeal Association," promised its protection against the legal consequences of his violence and misconduct, told me to my face, after he had been informed by myself that I was a Catholic priest—that if I should presume to take the chair at a meeting of the Irish Universal Suffrage Association, he would seize me by the neck, and drag me out of it, even if I were clothed in my robes.

Now, Sir, permit me to ask you when such a threat has been made to a priest, what is a layman to expect from such characters, particularly when they are encouraged in it by an association upon whose protection they rely with the most implicit confidence?

I am your obedient Servant,
P . Ryan .
Donabate, August 12, 1841.

Sophia Evans had never involved herself overly much with her husband's tenants and had rarely allowed the world beyond the borders of her demesne to overly intrude on the largely self-contained life she lived within it. The farm, and the house, were her kingdom and her laboratory and, within their lofty confines, she had lived a largely content and happy life, finding collegiality, authority, and a much-needed sense of purpose in the running of the family farm.

Family assets beyond the house and farm, however, had always been George's domain. She had rarely, if ever, sought to trespass on that. Rents and leases were troublesome matters, and unpleasantly feudal. She hadn't much stomach for that. *That*, had always been the sole responsibility of her husband. *That*, had always been man's work.

Following George's death, however, the task of setting and collecting rents still had to be done and as her land steward, William Kelly, a man known to have Tenant Right and Repeal sympathies, was at that time considered unwilling, or unsuited, to doing it, she had turned for help to a certain Edward Wolstenholme, a close friend. It was to prove one of the biggest mistakes of her life for Wolstenholme would set himself to the task with reckless enthusiasm.

In late January 1846, the Rev. Patrick Ryan allowed a 'Tenant Right' petition to be placed on a table at the door of the parish church in Donabate, where many of Sophia's tenants were alleged to have signed it. At this point, tensions between various factions in Irish politics were approaching boiling point. Chartists within the Repeal movement were very much engaged in an internal struggle that was leaching working-class support away from O'Connell. The country, furthermore, was just six months away from the Young Ireland expulsion from the Repeal Association for their refusal to renounce the use of violence. Editorials in the *Nation* newspaper, furthermore, were growing ever more militaristic in tone.

On hearing of the petition, Wolstenholme set out to discover who, if any, of Sophia's tenants or employees had signed it. When he discovered, or at the very least was led to believe, that a teacher at Sophia's boys' school had done so, he promptly fired him and issued threats against any other tenants who might be thinking of signing that, or any other, Chartist petition.

The teacher, who may or may not have been a member of the local Chartist organisation, had been employed by Sophia for seventeen years without any cause for concern or complaint. Well regarded locally, his sacking, for having had the temerity to exercise his constitutional right to sign a petition to parliament, inevitably caused all manner of upset and excitement in the village. The temperature was hardly lowered when it was later alleged that the teacher hadn't actually signed the petition.

The atmosphere in the village had now become so volatile and dangerous that the schoolhouse had to be closed. Enquiries were also reportedly made regarding the availability of extra police to keep the peace should cooler heads not prevail. In Sophia's absence, Wolstenholme had overstepped the mark, not just of his agency, but of propriety, and his intervention was to have an almost immediate effect on the life of William Kelly.

At the height of this bad feeling, one opportunistic tenant decided to try and land William Kelly, a prominent member of the local Repeal Association, in hot water with his mistress. Despite his religious, Tenant Right, and Repeal affiliations, Kelly was far from universally popular with Sophia's tenants, especially those who had thus far been resistant to his efforts to modernise local agricultural practices and turn 'bad' land into good. One must assume that he would also have been unpopular with those who supported the Chartist philosophy of their parish priest.

For a long time, many of Sophia Evans' tenants had been arguing for rent reductions on the basis that the land that they were leasing from her was poor and unproductive when compared to that elsewhere on the peninsula. Kelly, however, was forever undermining their case by achieving record yields on the same land and winning regular prizes at the Royal Dublin Society for his employer. Seen very much as Sophia's right-hand man, and an ardent supporter of O'Connell, there was bound to be a reaction when the petition crisis broke. It came, eventually, in the form of a poison-pen letter:

'Madam,

The kindness which I often experienced at the hand of your late excellent husband combined with a high personal regard for yourself, compels me at the risque of great pecuniary loss to put you on your guard with respect to a low cunning insidious man of the name of Kelly a member of this association (the Repeal).

He has recently boasted that he will ere long host a Repeal meeting in your drawing room and his plan of operation is to sow dissension between you and your tenantry so as to force you to leave Portrane and let the domain and house to him. He has compelled most of your tenants to become subscribed to the Repeal fund and of course associates. Just question them quietly upon this subject and then examine Kelly himself.

A friend.'

Kelly suddenly began to fear for his job, and indeed for his life. He became convinced that he was being set up to take flak from both Wolstenholme and those angry tenants who felt that he was far too loyal to O'Connell and, indeed, to the woman they believed was directing Wolstenholme's actions. To add further fuel to the fire, Wolstenholme was now being touted by some as being a German, even though his family had been settled in Ireland for several generations and had come from old Anglo-Saxon stock, and further accused, in the pages of the Northern Star, of having lured the teetotalling schoolteacher into a pub on the pretext of paying him his salary while his bailiffs emptied and took possession of his cottage.

As the rhetoric ratcheted up, William Kelly applied for a licence for two pistols to defend himself and his wife, and was, at least initially, refused. Feeling isolated and vulnerable in his cottage at Middlefield, he wrote to Sophia indicating that he would have to leave her employment and take his wife to a place of safety if their security could not be guaranteed at Middlefield. Unwilling to lose Kelly, Sophia hopped on the first boat back to Dublin and intervened on Kelly's behalf. Kelly got his licence and kept his job.

When Sophia heard about Wolstenholme's treatment of her long-serving schoolteacher, she attempted to remedy matters. But the teacher, by now, had had enough. He opted to leave immediately, with a year's salary in lieu of wages. The exact nature of the negotiations that led to his departure are unclear, but what we do know is that Sophia Evans had never, either before or after this incident, shown any intolerance of socialist philosophies, especially when couched in democratic and non-violent principles. The fact that O'Connell was so vehemently opposed to the Chartists might even have provoked in her some small degree of sympathy for their cause, for just three years later she would be writing quite admiringly to her nephew, Henry, about the ideas of a French utopian socialist called Henri Blanc.

The Chartist movement would more or less fizzle out in Ireland over the following years and, in 1848, the Chartist Priest, Patrick Ryan, would be granted permission to retire as the parish priest of Donabate on a pension of £20 a year. The grounds for his retirement would be given as 'infirmity'. He would be replaced by Fr. John McCarthy. Kelly remained, for the time being, as Sophia Evans' steward, and very much involved in agrarian politics.

KELLY'S FAMINE BREAD

BEYOND PORTRANE, OUT in the greater Fingal, the winter of 1846-1847 saw the malnourished falling victim to typhoid and local relief committees having to be established to prevent an epidemic and mass starvation. 'Private charity,' wrote Andrew Kettle, a friend of William Kelly and a witness to the crisis in nearby Swords, 'ceased to a large extent, as every clan seemed to have grown selfish in self-defence'.

Back in November, when the Relief Commission wrote to all local relief committees requiring them to ensure that able-bodied men worked at least eight hours each day, they had insisted that even the sick and disabled should be 'occupied to the extent of their ability' before receiving aid. The directive ran completely contrary to Government policy, which was to provide food outside of the workhouse without the requirement to work. It forced a lot of people outdoors that had no business being there, with tragic consequences.

The winter proved to be one of the coldest in living memory. Snow, frost, and icy gales sent the cost of food and fuel soaring. If the poor could find enough money to buy food, they often could not afford the necessary fuel to cook it, leading to the establishment of both charitable and government-funded soup kitchens. The rationale behind the kitchens was that by providing pre-cooked meals the kitchens would keep food prices down, reduce crime and allow the poor to return to the fields to grow crops again. Some were set up by the state purely to feed the hungry thousands. Others, however, were established by evangelical missionaries who saw starvation as a potential weapon of conversion.

The most cost-effective means of providing food relief, it was quickly found, was to import cheap poor-quality maize or 'Indian meal' from Britain's Indian colonies. Daily survival rations were set at a pound of meal per day for adults, and half a pound of meal per day for children. The meal was generally ground and added to warm water, but Kelly, having had his attention drawn to a recent newspaper article by Sophia Evans concerning the experiments of a Viennese baker with wheat and beetroot, suspected it could be more effectively used.

Kelly began to experiment, mixing varying quantities of Indian meal with cheaper crops like turnips, parsnips, and mangelwurzel. He felt duty-bound to do so, not just because it was his employer's suggestion, but because it was what his education had prepared him for.

'... I tried several experiments in making bread, from the different field root crops, in combination with wheaten and oaten meal, the results of which I communicated, at that time, to the Royal Dublin Society.

In my experiments I found that 10lbs of turnips yielded matter capable of being made into bread, with an equal weight of wheatmeal, only 2 lbs 10oz.; 10 lbs of mangelwurzel yielded of like matter 3 lbs.; 10 lbs. of parsnips yielded 6 lbs.; 10 lbs. of carrots 5 lbs. 10 oz. ... Each of these roots will assist, in the proportion already stated, to make very good bread.

The mangel wurzel is prepared for bread by grating the root, the pressing the pulp so as to render it sufficiently dry to combine with an equal weight of meal into bread; the turnip is then boiled and pressed; the carrot and parsnip are first slightly boiled, then peeled, when they are again boiled, then mashed fine and pressed the same way as the turnip.

It is a question whether there is any economy in converting any of these roots into bread, unless mangel wurzel, which cannot be used as human food in any other way.'

The crop Kelly finally settled on was mangelwurzel, or mangold, a type of beet grown primarily for livestock feed. This plant had begun life in Germany as *mangold-wurzel*, literally 'root of the beet', but this was apparently misheard as *mangel-wurzel* or 'root of scarcity'. The latter translation made its way to France as *racine de disette* and, in the previous century, an English translation of a French work by the Abbé de Commerell had introduced this plant to the English-speaking world by the same name. Drawn by the etymologically suspect nomenclature to the possible use of the plant for human consumption, Kelly had acted with the irresistible urge of the visionary.

Kelly's bread proved popular and within weeks it was in 'extensive use' locally. On 12 December 1846, he offered samples to the Practical Agricultural Association and seven days later, on 19 December, to the Royal Dublin Society. Here, with Sir Robert Kane in the chair, the secretary would read what he described as a 'very important paper' from Mr William

Kelly to a sectional meeting of the organisation:

'Gentlemen – About a fortnight since there appeared in most of the Dublin newspapers an account of a discovery said to have been made by a baker at Vienna – viz., making bread from a mixture of wheaten flour and garden beet root, in which it is said he was eminently successful. Now, I must say that the merit of a discovery should scarcely be given in this case to the baker of Vienna, because bread has been made in England, and even in Ireland, many years ago of wheatenmeal and turnips in equal parts, as well as of meal and potatoes; and taking beet instead of turnips or potatoes can scarcely be called a discovery. My attention having been directed to this subject a few days ago by Mrs Evans, it occurred to me that if the Vienna baker succeeded in making good bread of wheaten meal and garden beet, that we must, even in Ireland, succeed in making good bread of wheaten meal and mangel-wurzel, and I accordingly tried the experiment, in which I flatter myself I have also been eminently successful.

I take the liberty, gentlemen, of sending you a specimen of the bread. It is made and baked on the griddle exactly in the same way as the people in this part of the country make their whole meal bread; so that every cottager is certain to have made in his own family just as good an article of food from the same materials.

I have, with all my family, used the same bread as the specimen I send you at dinner exclusively for the last four days, and I esteem it highly; and, if my estimate of it be just, I think it a subject of the greatest importance at the present time.

The cake which I take the liberty of sending you, gentlemen, is composed of exactly 2½ lbs. of wheaten meal, 2½ lbs. of mangel-wurzel, with a little barm and salt. It weights exactly 4¾ lbs. so that the weight of the barm and salt is lost by evaporation in baking.

Yellow Globe Mangel Wurzel

The mangel-wurzel is cleaned and grated on a dish, and then let drain on a colander or hair sieve. A large portion of the juice thus drains off, which takes a great part of the nutritive matter of the root with it, I suppose. I was anxious, however, to have the bread made exactly with equal portions of the mangel root and meal; but, if the juice were all retained, it would take a considerably greater proportion of wheat meal to bring it to its proper consistence for bread. I, therefore, had the liquid drained off.

It is a fact, with which I am well acquainted, that cattle will thrive better on food composed of a mixture of beans and roots, or oats and roots (viz. turnips and mangel), than on either of these grains or roots separately. Hence it is possible that this bread is more nourishing than bread made exclusively of wheatenmeal.

If it be found to be good bread, then, viewing it as an article of economy, it will stand thus – one cwt. Of wheatenmeal will cost, at present, 18s.; a cwt. Of mangel wurzel will cost 1s.; so that the poor man, suppose him to buy 2 cwt. of bread, can get 1 cwt. For 18s., and the other cwt. For 1s.; that is, he can get as much mixed bread for 19s. as he could get wheaten bread for 36s.

It is true that a stone of wheatenmeal makes 18lbs. of bread, when manufactured exactly as this cake I send you has been; but the reason is obvious, it takes more than 4lbs. of water to make 14lbs. of meal into bread; but there is very little nutriment in water, so that I thinks there is much real gain by the increased weight.

There is a large quantity of mangel wurzel in this country that could be available for human food in this way this season, and if by directing attention to this subject that I can, in the remotest degree, be the means of saving even one human being from hunger, I shall be happy indeed.

I am, gentlemen,

most respectfully,
your very obedient, humble servant,
William Kelly,
Steward to Mrs Evans.

Kelly's letter was reprinted the following week in *The Farmer's Gazette*, from where it was subsequently picked up by the national press. In the course of reporting on Kelly's article, the Gazette credited Kelly with being the first man to 'have made known the use of mangel in the shape of bread. The Gazette further credited him with:

'... the merit of having grown the heaviest crop of mangelwurzel on record – namely, 90 tons per acre on land similar to which are thousands of acres in Ireland at present comparatively valueless, but which could be made, by the application of well-expended capital, by well-directed skill, such as Mr Kelly has brought to bear on Mrs Evans' property at Portrane, to produce the finest crops of mangel, oats, turnips, Italian rye grass, and, perhaps, wheat and barley.

Yes, there are thousands of acres in Ireland capable of all this if in the hands of such a proprietress as Mrs Evans, and managed by such a man as Mr Kelly, thereby affording an immense amount of employment – producing abundance of such crops, followed by oats, clover, and turnips in due course – adding immeasurably to the people's food and the nation's wealth.'

The average working man, Kelly calculated, was consuming 4lbs of potatoes in a single meal. Figures from German scientific journals, however, were showing mangelwurzel to be as high in nutrients, as potatoes; perhaps even more so. However it may have tasted, Kelly's mangelwurzel bread, and the undoubted reason for its 'extensive use' around Donabate and Portrane during the famine years, was that it was nutritious and cost half as much as wheaten bread to make. Offering a significant saving to the household budget of the poor, it gave them the financial space to purchase other foods.

Whatever else William Kelly would go on to achieve in his lifetime, this bread, his employment of local children in preference to sowing machines, his dogged preference for manual tilling over ploughing, and his swiftness in grasping an opportunity to reclaim land and grow green crops unaffected by the blight, would help in no small or uncertain manner to save many families in his local community from destitution and death during the Great Famine. It was a significant contribution, worthy in itself of recognition and remembrance, but Kelly wasn't finished yet.

SOUP AND SALVATION

IN NOVEMBER 1846, cognisant of what was happening at Portrane, the members of the newly formed Practical Agricultural Society (sometimes called the Irish Farmers' Association) asked William Kelly to prepare and present a paper on 'the varieties and cultivation of such crops as are likely to prove the best substitute for the potato'.

Kelly presented his paper at midday on Tuesday, 1 December 1846, at their premises in Northumberland Buildings in Dublin. Titled, *'The crops proper to be grown at this emergency, and their culture'*, it was published in full in *The Farmer's Gazette* and reported in detail five days later in the *Leinster Express*.

The Practical Agricultural Society was essentially an offshoot of *The Farmer's Gazette*, and very much the brainchild of Edward Purdon, joint proprietor of the paper. Purdon had long been a supporter of skilled agriculturists from humble backgrounds like William Kelly and Thomas Skilling. Impressed by Kelly's paper, Purdon had an idea. He approached Kelly again. Would he, given the current crisis, be willing to collate his ideas on how to prevent a national catastrophe in a single book for urgent publication. Kelly agreed.

As a result of this request, and no doubt a deal of financial assistance from Purdon, William Kelly published, in January 1847, his *'Irish Small Farmer of 1847; Containing Ample Directions for the Cultivation of the Soil During the Present Crisis'*. Aimed at helping small tenant farmers move away from their reliance on the potato and into the cultivation of alternative crops, it took the same cost-benefit approach as his previous book and repeated much of what he had already written in articles for *The Farmer's Gazette.*

On this occasion, however, Kelly chose to deal with a wider variety of subjects: food and labour economy, land reclamation and drainage, manure making and application, tillage, crop rotation and management, the comparative merits of crops for cattle and people, calf rearing and cow feeding, dairy management, garden crops, beekeeping, and cottage economy. In other words, his grand ideas writ small.

The book/pamphlet, which retailed at tuppence a copy, was advertised in the small ads on the front page of the *Dublin Evening Post* as being of interest to the 'agricultural classes.' It was available, furthermore, at ALL booksellers, suggesting that Purdon was also assisting with its distribution.

The pamphlet was well-received and enormously influential. Just four months after its publication many of Kelly's ideas were being quoted in *'Plain and Useful Hints for Farmers'*, by a Mr J. Judge, from Youghal in Co. Cork. The timing was perfect for Kelly's book, but it had competition. A rival publication on the same subject was being simultaneously published by the Scottish agriculturist, James Clapperton.

Clapperton's book was sponsored by the rival Royal

Agricultural Improvement Society of Ireland, an organisation consisting almost exclusively of the nobility and landed gentry. Though aware of Kelly's work – he mentions Kelly's mangelwurzel bread in his book – Clapperton's book was nevertheless far less detailed and somewhat condescending in tone. Lacking in an understanding of its target audience, it failed to make quite the same impact amongst them.

Kelly, in many ways the very quintessence of Victorian propriety, still managed to write with the calloused hand of a man as familiar with the practice of farming as the theory of it; a man who knew the weight, measure, and cost of everything he recommended. He appeared to understand, as if from personal experience, the economy of small farms and the realities of life upon them. He also enjoyed the advantage that his surname would identify him as one of their own. He was Irish, plain-speaking, and Catholic. A man with black crescents under his fingernails. Elizabeth Kelly's investment in her son's education had paid off, not just for her, but perhaps also for the country at large.

By the summer of 1847, three-quarters of a million labourers were engaged in public works schemes and the soup kitchens were overwhelmed by the scale of the destitution. People were dying in their thousands.

Amongst the casualties in the city were Michael and Mary Jane 'May' Derrick of Liffey Street in Dublin. May Derrick had stood as godmother at the baptism of Mary Jane Kelly's niece in 1835. Both Mary Jane Kelly and May Derrick's maiden names had also been Shanks. It is likely, therefore, that they were closely related, most probably cousins. Mary Jane Kelly would, therefore, have known the Derricks reasonably well.

It is not known how May Derrick died, only that her death preceded that of her husband, Michael, a Sligo-born plasterer. Michael died at the North Dublin Union Workhouse on 12 June 1847, having been admitted on 29 June of the previous year in a state of 'delicate health'. His nine-year-old daughter, also called Mary Jane, had at that stage been taken in by James Shanks to be raised alongside his own daughter. She was twelve years of age at the time. The two Mary Jane's would be raised as sisters.

This all begs the obvious question: how did Michael Derrick end up dying in the workhouse when his wife's namesake and close relative was living on a farm in north County Dublin where food and work were plentiful and her husband was devoting so much of his time and energy into ensuring that the tenant farmers and labourers of Ireland did not starve? Was it pride, or something else that stopped him from seeking help before the workhouse became his only option?

Michael Derrick had married May Shanks thirteen years prior to the Kellys' wedding, on 15 April 1823. They'd had a son, Matthew, who was born in 1825, and were still alive in 1838, when May Derrick, as she was now called, gave birth to a daughter, also named Mary Jane. The clue to any possible estrangement and the unusually long gap between their two children may well be explained by an article in the *Dublin Evening Packet* of 14 October 1828.

On that day, Michael Derrick was listed in the legal reports amongst those charged with insolvency in the Dublin Debtor's Court. People convicted of insolvency at that time were typically left to rot in prison until such time as their debts were paid. The fact that Michael Derrick was free in 1837 would suggest that someone paid his debts. A prolonged term of imprisonment would also go a long way towards explaining his subsequent destitution and 'delicate health'.

In 1835 Eliza Shanks (née Barrett), wife of Mary Jane Kelly's brother, James, had also given birth to a daughter called Mary Jane. She was baptised on 13 December 1835 at St. James' Church in Dublin and standing as her godmother on that cold winter's day was Michael Derrick's wife, May. It is possible, therefore, that May Derrick had been living with James and Eliza Shanks while her husband was in prison.

William Kelly was a famously moral and charitable man. At a later date, when young Mary Jane Derrick needed his help, he would open his home to her, and would similarly offer both home and gainful employment to other, more distant, relatives of his own from County Monaghan.

It is unlikely, therefore, that the problem lay at his end, and yet there are so many possibilities, on all sides, for familial conflict when money is involved. We can only speculate. All we know for certain is that Michael and May Derrick died and that it was James Shanks who took in their daughter, and not his childless sister, Mary Jane Kelly, who was perhaps better placed to do so.

Despite the widespread starvation, there was no shortage of food in the country. Forty to seventy shiploads of food sailed from Ireland's ports each day protected by 100,000 troops plus police, navy, and coastguard. The starving poor could only stand and watch.

Throughout Fingal, three and a half thousand people a day were queuing up with their penny tickets at local soup kitchens (trading one ticket for bread and another for soup). On any given day, up in Dublin, there were as many as five thousand queuing to be fed at the temporary kitchens that had been set up by the authorities on The Croppies' Acre, just outside the gates of the Royal Barracks.

The Croppies' Acre soup kitchen was being run by a French chef, Alexis Soyer, who had been approached by the authorities to set up a model kitchen to feed the starving poor at an economically viable cost. Thirty-eight-year-old Soyer, the renowned chef and designer of the Reform Club kitchen in London, managed to make his soup at a cost of just £1 for every 100 gallons and to feed people in shifts of 100 at a time, the end of each shift being marked by the ringing of a bell.

Soyer's 'Model Soup Kitchen' proved controversial in some quarters, however, as Soyer insisted on charging public figures and upper-class voyeurs the princely sum of five shillings a head to watch the poor being fed. Comparisons were made in the national press to the nearby Zoological Gardens, where one could watch the animals being fed for just sixpence a head. Nevertheless, at its peak, the kitchen was feeding almost 9,000 people per day, the model proving so successful that Soyer would repeat it for soldiers during the Crimean war. By July, across the entire country, almost three million people were, on a daily basis, being fed at soup kitchens of one form or another.

Down in Portrane, however, one could almost have pretended that the famine did not exist. No one was dying from hunger and the peninsula was largely free of disease. And though some attributed the health of the community to the presence of holy wells, at that time the generosity of Mrs Sophia Evans and the work of her a Monaghan-born steward, were generally credited as being the cause.

'My body to Ireland, my heart to Rome, and my soul to heaven.' Such, allegedly, were the parting words of 'The Liberator', Daniel O'Connell, as he lay on his death bed at the Hotel Feder in Genoa. It was 9.37 p.m. on Saturday, 15 May 1847, and O'Connell had been travelling on a pilgrimage to Rome. He had fallen ill in Marseille but, refusing to listen to his physician, had ploughed on to Genoa where he finally succumbed to a 'softening of the brain'. Such was his reputation throughout Europe that on the night of his demise the clergy of the local Cathedral walked in a torchlight procession through the city to be present at his deathbed.

In accordance with his wishes, and indeed his monstrous self-regard, O'Connell's heart was removed during the embalming process and placed in a silver urn. Father John Miley, O'Connell's chaplain, had intended to take the urn to St. Peter's Basilica in Rome, but the Vatican had other ideas.

In his youth O'Connell had been somewhat contemptuous of the faith, only to zealously reconvert in later life. As a result, he had never entirely managed to allay Vatican suspicions that he was 'unorthodox in religion'. Furthermore, during the recently ended First Carlist War in Spain, O'Connell had publicly declared himself in favour of the more liberal regency side rather than the ultra-Catholic Carlists. Poor Miley, unsurprisingly, struggled to persuade Saint Peter's to accept the urn and, in the end, the only place that would take it off his hands was the church of the Irish College, Saint Agata dei Goti, from where it would mysteriously disappear sometime in the early years of the 20th century.

So much for O'Connell's heart. His body, on the other hand, would eventually be placed in a lead coffin, encased in hardwood, and shipped to Dublin where, with much pomp and ceremony, it would finally be laid to rest at Glasnevin, in the cemetery that he himself had established in 1832. The cemetery committee, whose members were largely drawn from O'Connell's Catholic Association, had appealed to the O'Connell family for the body and paid for it to be returned from Italy.

Glasnevin Cemetery

The cemetery at Glasnevin was never more prominent in the minds of nationalist Catholics as it was in the summer of 1847 when a nation awaited the return of its hero, a man whose legacy was already beginning to emerge in a generation of young nationalists who, inspired by the country's Gaelic past, were being incited to radicalism by the famine. Led by the prominent Protestant activist, Thomas Davis, they would soon take up arms in yet another failed attempt to make their homeland 'a nation once again'.

Elizabeth Kelly never lived to see the grand spectacle that was to be Daniel O'Connell's funeral, for she beat him to the cemetery by just twenty-two days.

On 12 July, she passed away at the Kellys' cottage at Middlefield. She was 86. She died in the certain knowledge that her son would be the last of his line. Mary Jane was now fifty years of age. She had given William so much, but perhaps not the gift that Elizabeth had most wanted for her son.

Elizabeth was buried, not in Donabate or Portrane, but in the Garden Section of Prospect Cemetery in Glasnevin, just a stone's throw from the spot where O'Connell's grave lay waiting for him under the vigilant gaze of the night watchmen who guarded fresh corpses against the work of resurrectionists. Kelly paid for the plot. In time, it would serve as his own.

Ten days after O'Connell's funeral, every soup kitchen in Fingal was closed. To general consternation, those that ran them were threatened with police action should they fail to comply. A financial crisis in England had forced the government to tighten its purse strings. The kitchens had been in operation for just six months.

To add to the woes of the poor, the potato harvest, though successful, had failed to yield enough potatoes to feed the population through the coming winter. Grain prices had fallen, but food prices remained beyond the wages of those on public works. An entire social class sat teetering on the precipice of disaster. Beyond the Portrane peninsula, starvation levels began to increase and diseases like cholera and typhoid began to spread.

The Poor Law Commissioners, opposed to outdoor relief, now insisted that all able-bodied men should work eight hours a day in the stone breakers yards to qualify for food relief. Furthermore, under the infamous Gregory Clause, any small farmer holding more than a quarter of an acre of land was now obliged to surrender his land in order to seek public assistance. In the Fingal area alone, two hundred and twenty small farmers lost their farms. 'Gregoryism' quickly became a byword for eviction, exile, and death. It had been a summer in which only the weather could be said to have been pleasant.

The autumn started quietly. The apples were harvested from the orchards, the chestnuts had turned golden brown and the grey seals paid their usual visit with their pups to the Rogerstown Estuary whenever the sea was calm. The darkening mornings marked as peaceful a change of season as had ever been seen in Portrane and a darkening mood in the world beyond.

Observing the sea on three sides, was almost the same as four. It created an island mentality in Portrane and a sense of isolation that was not always to its detriment. And yet, despite all of the digging and trenching, despite the dearth of idle hands, there was something in the air; something intangible, a sense that yet another 'agitation' was hatching.

It all kicked off in October, when John Mitchel, an Ulster Protestant, began to urge the tenants of Ireland to withhold their agricultural produce for their own consumption. The following December he would go even further, suggesting that they arm themselves in preparation for a war between the forces of property and poverty.

Over the course of that autumn and winter, at least six landlords and ten farm managers would be murdered. With the soup kitchens closed, and the workhouses full to overcrowding, the desperation of the poor had reached boiling point. The country was heading for yet another armed rebellion; a rebellion that was doomed to explode like a damp firework during the summer of 1848.

Despite the paramilitary posturing of the country at large, however, people were generally too busy in Portrane to take much notice. Under William Kelly's direction, the Evans estate was engaged in labour-intensive agriculture that, to the astonishment of many, still managed to turn a profit. The local inhabitants were not blind to what was happening in the outside world, nor, it seems, were outsiders blind to what was happening at Portrane. In September 1847, a front-page article in the *Irish Examiner* saw an anonymous Corkonian rhapsodising the relief work of Sophia Evans:

'Ballyphehane, if reclaimed, is capable of producing as good crops of every kind as those grown on similar land by Mrs Evans of Portrane, in the county Dublin. The name of Portrane is now associated with the history of the improved agriculture of Europe, aye, and America, too. Cannot government, or a public body with a suitable staff, do that which a widow lady did by the aid of one practical Irishman?'

William Kelly wasn't mentioned by name, but he no longer needed to be. Every literate farmer in the country knew by now who the 'practical Irishman' was. By January of the following year, Kelly's latest book would have proved so popular and influential that the *Agricultural Journal and Transactions of the Lower Canada Agricultural Society* would be quoting from a 'fifth edition'. Five editions in two years!

Kelly's advice, on all matters agricultural, had by now become a treasured national resource and his self-invented raised-bed system of cultivating green crops had achieved such popular acclaim that, by February 1848, the *United Irishman* newspaper would be declaring that:

'The drill bed-sowing system, now called the "Kellyan system" has been so often described, that we need not do more than merely mention it.'

This system, as mentioned before, involved the growing of green crops in raised beds and providing the plants with a greater depth of soil in places where such depth did not naturally exist. It enabled farmers to obtain heavy crops from an otherwise thin and indifferent piece of ground.

Later that same year, a report by Kelly to the Royal Dublin Society on the crop rotation of mangelwurzel, was referenced by Philip Digwell in his book '*Modern Agriculture as peculiarly applicable to Ireland, including draining, sub-soiling, manuring, rotation of crops, and house-feeding*'. In their work together, Sophia Evans and William Kelly had, in their own small way, placed Portrane at the heart of a significant, if short-lived, agricultural revolution.

THE IRISH SMALL FARMER OF 1847

IT MAY WELL have been as much a work of agricultural economics as a textbook on holistic and organic farming, but William Kelly's ground-breaking publication, *The Irish Small Farmer of 1847*, contained nothing that he had not already successfully and publicly implemented at Portrane, and nothing that was not plainly stated in language that could be understood by even semi-literate farmers.

Championed and distributed with the aid of Edward Purdon, joint owner of *The Farmer's Gazette*, it deserves a special place in the history of Irish agriculture for both its ambition and influence. It opened, however, to the surprise of many, with a treatise on horses.

In Ireland at that time there were approximately half a million farms under fifteen statute acres, keeping a stock of a quarter of a million horses and mules. During a famine, Kelly asserted, this was nothing short of madness. He had no problem with the use of horses on larger farms, indeed he had recommended as much in his previous book. But on farms of less than fifteen acres, he now argued, the possession of a horse had become a luxury that no small farmer could afford.

The argument regarding the use of horses was nothing new. His old mentor, the Rev. William Hickey, had touched upon it in 1830 in his *Hints for the Small Farmers of Ireland,* a work written under the pseudonym of 'Martin Doyle'. But Kelly had taken Hickey's suggestion to another level entirely. By analysing everything the horse contributed to, and consumed on, the farm, he demonstrated clearly and concisely how the rising cost of grains meant that the cost of a horse now far outweighed the benefits.

The possibility of total reliance on the potato had gone forever, and the expensive wheat and oats that had previously been sold to pay the landlord were now being increasingly consumed by the tenant and his family. But on the majority of small farms, the greatest consumer of oats was not, in fact, the family, but their horse. This, Kelly argued, was unsustainable in the current circumstances. Even a donkey would be a better option if an animal was deemed absolutely essential for farm transport. As for tillage, he further advised, on all farms of fifteen acres or less this could, and should, now be done by hand, i.e. with the spade and not with a horse-drawn plough.

Taking just 7lbs of oats per horse per day as an estimate of consumption, an estimate he readily admitted was seriously and unrealistically low, Kelly calculated a saving to the Irish economy of 128,504 stone of oats per day if small farmers were to switch to manual tilling. That was more than enough, he claimed, should those oats be ground into oatmeal, to provide a nutritious daily breakfast to 1.5 million

THE

IRISH SMALL FARMER

OF

1847;

CONTAINING AMPLE DIRECTIONS

FOR THE CULTIVATION OF THE SOIL

DURING THE PRESENT CRISIS.

BY WILLIAM KELLY,

STEWARD TO MRS. EVANS, PORTRANE, COUNTY DUBLIN.

Author of "A TREATISE ON VILLA FARMS," &c.

Published at the request of

"The Irish Farmer's Association."

DUBLIN:

CUMMING & FERGUSON, LOWER ORMOND QUAY,

AGENTS for the Sale of the JOURNALS of

"THE ROYAL AGRICULTURAL SOCIETY OF ENGLAND;"

"THE HIGHLAND SOCIETY OF SCOTLAND;" ETC.

TWO PENCE.

working men!

At a time when people were starving on account of their reliance on potatoes, he further asserted, the possession of horses by small farmers represented:

'... an absolute injury to their owners, because when the horse is on the farm, the tillage will certainly be done by the animal, and the horse not being well fed, the tillage must certainly be bad, – thus making the unfortunate owner of the horse sustain a double loss ... A horse on a small farm is a dead loss, equal to the amount of his keep, as well as the difference between a good crop, consequent on good tillage with the spade, and a bad crop, consequent on bad tillage by a badly fed horse; and it would not, by any means, be an over estimate to calculate that abundant food, three times a day, for upwards of a million of working men, is lost annually, merely by keeping horses on small farms.'

Even at one shilling and sixpence a day, Kelly argued, the cost of a farm labourer was less than the cost of having the land properly tilled by horses, though he allowed it really depended on the nature of the soil and the standard rate for farm labourers in the locality. He had himself recently switched to using local labourers in the preparation of difficult land for the cultivation of parsnips and the resultant crop yields had more than compensated for the increased employment. His preference for manual tilling, furthermore, had meant that the labourers of Portrane had become neither migrant nor vagrant, as they had elsewhere in Fingal, nor had the local economy collapsed. As he had learned at Bannow, the most effective form of education was example. Nothing was copied quicker than success.

This advice represented a complete reversal of the advice he had offered to the wealthy owners of small to medium-sized farms back in 1836 when he wrote:

'All crops should be sown and otherwise managed, as far as convenient, with the plough; and no spade work permitted, in planting potatoes or putting in other crops, where the plough can possibly be used.'

But back then he was talking directly to the wealthy owners of good land at a time when the cost of grains was not so high. Now he was speaking to poor farmers with poor quality land at a time when the cost of grains had rocketed. He was not being hypocritical or opportunistic, he was merely matching the solution to the specific economic problem. Farms were businesses. Farmers had to be pragmatic. On land that was capable of being drained, Kelly offered detailed instructions on undersoil drainage. On land that was not, he advised farmers to look instead to ascertaining what crops could be grown on such land in the summer months when the land was not waterlogged.

Kelly's favourite topic, however, like Arthur Young before him, was chemistry, and in particular the manufacture of manure. On this, he shared his personal formulas for mixing and offered figures detailing the increase in crop yields he had achieved with each individual mix. He even dared to suggest that landlords supply the manure to their tenants at cost price or on credit, as the resulting yield increases would more than make up for the initial loss of income.

And then there was the controversial matter of burning. For a long time prior to the outbreak of the famine, Irish landlords had thought it necessary to have stringent clauses inserted into their tenants' leases, prohibiting them 'under pain and penalties' from burning any part of their land. They did this in the belief that burning destroyed the soil.

Kelly, however, argued for change. 'The soil,' he asserted, 'although converted into ashes, still remains almost in its entirety. Some fertilizing gases are expelled, but they are again absorbed from the atmosphere'. The danger, as Kelly saw it, was not from the use, but the abuse, of burning land. Where crops were repeatedly sown without any manure the land was always going to be damaged, but it was not the burning of it, he asserted, that was the cause. You got back from the land what you put into it. It was a simple equation.

But if his offerings on the subject of burning had appeared controversial to the small farmers of his day, then his offerings on the subject of human waste, or 'night soil', must have seemed positively heretical. At this time scarcely any small farmer in Ireland possessed such a thing as a toilet. Kelly, however, suggested the construction of outhouses in the shape of a sentry box that sat over a tank three feet deep and raised 12 inches above the ground. This, he claimed, could be done for as little as 18 shillings and could possibly be given as prizes to smallholders by local farming societies.

By adding burned earth, ashes from the house fires, sawdust, and other absorbent materials to human waste, Kelly asserted, the tank, when full, could be emptied and stored in a narrow heap in much the same way as ordinary farmyard manure. It is not known how many of the small farmers of Portrane followed Kelly's advice, but those who did, like Kelly himself, may well have been the first of their kind in Ireland to construct outside toilets.

The manure collected from human waste, Kelly went on, was ideal for green crops. If used correctly, it would save the small farmer the cost of expensive guano. His ideas on these matters had come from the land of pagodas and yellow emperors, where human waste was baked into cakes and applied to the land as a powder or in solution. They had also come from France where, with typical Gallic sensitivity, it was sold more delicately as *poudrette*. Its use, however, had thus far been shunned by Irish farmers who, quite literally, had turned up their noses at the very thought of it.

Continuing with the theme, Kelly also suggested the recycling of human and animal urine which, when augmented with slops from the house, could also be used as manure. Human urine, he claimed, was best, followed by that of the pig, then that of the cow. He showed how urine from the privy or barn could be routed to a tank by means of drains, and then diluted and applied to crops with a watering can or cask.

He had adapted this idea, he claimed, from the writings of Justus von Liebig, a forty-three-year-old German beginning to make a name for himself as the father of organic chemistry. Using von Liebig's calculations, Kelly estimated, the organic waste of a single human being could provide sufficient manure to fertilise an acre of land for the cultivation of wheat, oats, or rye. Again, a significant cost saving to the small farmer.

One of Kelly's most startling claims was that by following his method of crop rotation it would be possible, on just a single acre of land, to produce five barrels of wheat or eight barrels of oats, ten tons of mangelwurzel, one and a half barrels of beans, two and a half tons of parsnips or one ton of potatoes. Such yields, of course, would be entirely dependent upon manual tilling and the spreading of manure in accordance with his stated principles. The same system would also supply sufficient garden vegetables to feed a family of five for a year, providing that they also kept a cow.

His system worked in the following manner. At any given time, half of the holding had to be under wheat or oats, and the other half under green crops every alternate year, with the sole exception of the garden, which could remain stationary. This was achieved by ensuring that mangelwurzel was never grown on the same patch of ground more than once every four years, and beans and parsnips no more than once in every eight.

Thus, in the diagram below, in the second year mangelwurzel occupies box 3 and beans and parsnips boxes 1 and 2 respectively. In the third year, mangelwurzel occupies the place of potatoes and beans in year one and the latter crops box 3. In the fourth year, mangelwurzel occupies boxes 1 and 2 and, in the fifth year, they occupy the same box from whence they started the rotation etc. It was a simple plan, easily understood by any small farmer, and just as easily executed.

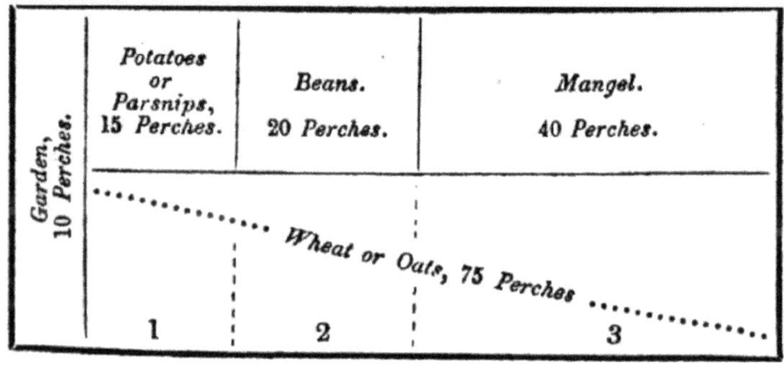

A detailed breakdown of how much of the crops were to be set aside for the family, and how much needed to be set aside exclusively for the animals, was provided. But the further pre-requisite to success was the use of Kelly's mangelwurzel bread to augment the family's nutrition, and the use of parsnips as a vegetable. Two pigs and a cow would also be necessary to be kept.

So detailed was the breakdown of costs that Kelly's advice could only have come from practical local knowledge. It suggests that at least some of the small tenant farmers of Portrane had already been using this method of rotation and had been able, as Kelly had famously claimed, to keep their families fed on a single acre and still have as many as 176 days free to engage in other paid employment, which at Portrane presumably included digging and trenching. Similar, but not identical, systems of crop rotation were provided for farms of five acres and for cottage gardens.

Regarding the failure of the potato crop, Kelly allowed that the replacement of it as a staple food could never be accomplished by any one individual crop. It could, however, be replaced by a unique combination of other specially selected vegetables i.e. wheat, oats, beans, and peas, from the grain crops, and mangelwurzel, turnips, carrots, and parsnips, from the root crops. His opinions on the best varieties of these crops were based on his own research and experimentation, the results of which, he claimed, had already been published in respectable agricultural journals.

Lazy Beds or Ridges

As already mentioned, Kelly was a big champion of

the practice of growing green crops in beds or ridges, a system that had already come to be known as the 'Kellyan' system. Like any scientist, he was happy to share his ideas, but he had lately been moved to rancour by the discovery that others could commit the monstrous solecism of reprinting them without attribution:

'This bed system was first practised by myself about 9 years ago, and I have continued the practice ever since with very great success. I perceive that newspaper editors and newspaper writers, from time to time latterly, have recommended this plan in a qualified degree; and land agents and gentlemen proprietors, taking the hint from the newspapers, I suppose, think well of recommending this practice to their tenantry, but to be practised only on wet lands.

Now this is what a certain Editor that I know would call "contemporary pilfering." However I will forgive the pilferers; gentlemen of the press, and gentlemen of the soil, will always be welcome to use any little discovery, or rather improvement, of mine without acknowledgement; but I will beg of them to give the system which they think well of recommending for practice, in certain cases, fair play; and, when they recommend it, I would beg of them to do so, not in the qualified condition of on wet soils, without showing, cause from practice, why it is not equal to drill culture on dry soils.'

Kelly completed his book by giving some money-saving recipes for 'Indian Meal Stirabout' and 'Rice Porridge', as well as some sage advice on the keeping of pigs and bees. His systems were practical, sometimes innovative, and perhaps still of interest to the modern allotment owner or organic farmer. If subsequent testimony in the national press during the middle years of the nineteenth century is to be believed, Kelly's innovations had quite a significant impact on agricultural practices, not just in Portrane, but in the country as a whole, both during *and* after the Great Famine.

ACROSS THE ATLANTIC

KELLY'S FAME, COURTESY of reports of his offerings to the journals of the Royal Dublin Society, began to cross the Atlantic. In January 1848, the *Agricultural Journal and Transactions of the Lower Canada Agricultural Society* republished a chapter on calf rearing and cow feeding from his latest book. By March they were reporting news of his presentation of some 60 varieties of wheat, 70 of oats, 26 of barley, and 'a very fine show of the indigenous grasses of Ireland' to the RDS Museum of Farm Produce.

William Kelly had come a long way from his days at the Bannow Farm School. He was now an agriculturist of some small fame and international influence. His work was being constantly referenced, even if he himself had by now gone largely silent.

In June the Canadians returned once again to Kelly

to report on his growing of parsnips and his methods of land reclamation and crop rotation:

Among others, some grown on ground belonging to Mrs Evans of Portrane, by Mr Kelly, her steward, weighed from twenty to twenty-six pound each. The crop, of which these were a sample, averaged from sixty to eighty tons per acre.

Mr Kelly, in his report to the society, says, that "these samples were sown on a moory bottom, the surface of which, in the year 1841, was a mass of rushes and other aquatic plants. The surface, to the depth of about four inches was completely burned, in the spring, and early part of the summer of that year; and the whole field, about eight acres, was sown without any manure but the ashes, with turnips, potatoes and mangel wurzel.

The mangel this year, from which the samples are sent, is growing where the potatoes grew last year. The seeds were sown on the 12th, 14th and 17th of May, in ridges five and a half feet wide; three rows in each ridge; plants eighteen inches asunder in the rows"

It would be a mistake to believe that Kelly's methods were designed solely to benefit the local community. He was a farmer first and foremost, and his livelihood was dependent upon his *profitable* management of the estate and tenants of Mrs Sophia Evans. But the undeniable truth of the matter was that it served neither tenant nor landlord well to have rents unpaid or crops unsold. The more productive the tenant, the healthier the estate, and indeed the community at large.

Their daily concerns were rarely so much in concert. Disease was no respecter of class. Labourers were hired as work became available, and if his tenant farmers suffered less during the famine because of his methods, then it was only as things should have been everywhere else. It saddened him greatly that it was not and, in his subsequent writings, one cannot escape the sense that he had come to believe that, had he been born into a different social class, his advice might have been heeded. The abundance of food on the estate, however, was not grown to be shared, but to be sold. The sharing of his systems was not an act of charity, but the offering of a neighbourly hand, as a teacher might guide his pupils to self-reliance.

Beyond Portrane, however, the abject misery persisted. Just 10km down the road, in the townland of Lusk, the population would fall by approximately twelve per cent in the decade between 1841 and 1851, with some 400 houses being demolished and a further 140 abandoned. A deputation of unemployed labourers from that same district had only recently complained to the guardians of the Balrothery workhouse that there were more than two hundred labourers currently unemployed in the parish. They had walked to Cashel and Mullingar in search of work on the railroads, only to be forced to return empty-handed 'after eating half our clothes'. Their wives and children were starving, their potatoes were all lost, and the farmers of Lusk had no work for them. Indeed, matters had so deteriorated in the wider Fingal area that in 1848 food distribution centres had to be set up throughout the district, including one in Donabate.

Spring came, the days lengthened, and the tenant farmers of Fingal finally roused themselves from their fatalistic languor. Following a public meeting in Swords, they became the first tenants in the country to attempt to 'bring the landlords to a sense of the altered state of things' by means of a campaign of public embarrassment. In the hope of forcing their landlords into a fair abatement of rents, they published their plight, and their resolutions, in the local and national newspapers.

The strategy proved moderately successful. Reductions were offered by many of the local landowners, with Sophia Evans' generosity meriting especial mention in the *London Express*:

'Mrs Evans of Portrane, whose charities to the poor have been so constant and liberal during the distress, has made an abatement of 20 per cent to her tenantry.'

And it wasn't just famine and disease that was causing the depopulation of Fingal. Under the Poor Law Acts, orphaned teenage girls were being sent to the colonies to *'help address the gender imbalance'*, the first being a group of ten girls sent from Swords to Australia in 1849. Another 73 people would be sent from Swords to Quebec in 1850.

On the Portrane peninsula, in stark contrast, the population would fall by just 10 people between 1841 and 1851. And down in Ballisk, a low-lying area of the peninsula described as a long, crooked street of squalid mud cabins peopled mostly by field labourers, things were no worse. Under the questionable administration of an absentee landlord, Ballisk had long endured poverty equal to the worst found anywhere in Ireland. The inhabitants were particularly vulnerable during times of flooding or heavy snow when 'a week was enough to bring them to the verge of starvation'.

In pockets of similarly crowded poor-quality housing elsewhere in the country, disease had become rampant. From a sample of 7,000 deaths from a similar area in West Cork in 1847, 44% had died of fever, 34% of starvation and 22% of dysentery. And yet, despite all of that, the disease-prone hovel at Ballisk would be described by Frances Power Cobbe as being, in 1851, 'one of those which suffered least in Ireland'.

Much, though not all, of this, was due to William Kelly's insistence on the use of manual labour where at all possible. Estate owners like Sophia Evans were the main source of employment in the Irish countryside and all manner of skilled and semi-skilled workers looked to them, and to each other, for work. By insisting on manual labour Kelly, who was effectively in sole charge of the estate during Sophia's many absences, kept many local labourers employed when there was no work to be found elsewhere, a fact that was obliquely referenced in 1849, in the journal of the Lower Canada Agricultural Society:

'We have seen a report of prizes awarded in November last by the Dublin Royal Society, at their Agricultural Museum – and the largest produce raised of the long red mangel-wurzel, was by Mrs Evans of Portrane, cultivated in ridges, with 50 tons of farm-yard manure, the after culture all done with the spade and hoe – and produce over 80 tons to the Irish acre.

The same lady got the first prize for the yellow globe mangel, cultivated in the same way, and having the same produce. Both were sown in the second week of May. She also obtained the first prize for carrots, of which the produce was over 60 tons to the Irish acre: manure, 3cwt of guano to the acre; cultivation, beds in rows twelve inches apart, plants 5 inches apart – sown 2nd May. Crop tilled exclusively with the spade, and the report states "the crops on the head lands which would be waste if the plough was used, would remunerate for the entire labour employed".

The lady took four prizes (all that were offered) for very great crops of beans and peas, which is a very good estimate of what a lady can do in the way of farming, and against such competitors as the Duke of Leinster, the Earls of Claremont and Meath, and many others of high rank. We give these results and modes of cultivation to show what may be done, and by persons who do not themselves hold the plough. We forgot to mention field cabbages: 50 tons farm-yard manure – sown 40 inches apart, 20th April – produced 95 tons to the Irish acre, as near as we can estimate from the number of barrels, 22 of 14 stone. Red wheat over 80, and white wheat nearly 80 bushels to the Irish acre.'

Mrs Evans took the plaudits, but the achievement was Kelly's. Later that same year, the Canadian journal would report again on Kelly's innovations in the growing of parsnips:

'Drill culture may also be adopted by the small farmer whose only implement is the spade. The drills may be raised by a shovel, a garden line being used to keep the drills straight and at equal distances apart. But by farmers of this class, it will be found more advisable to cultivate their parsnips and other green crops in beds, a mode originally introduced by Mr Kelly, of Portrane, and which is admirably adapted for green crop culture.

In following this method, the land is dug, or otherwise prepared in winter, as already described. In spring it receives another ploughing or digging and is then levelled and marked into beds four and a half feet wide, with a division of about eighteen inches by two feet (according to the depth of the soil) between each bed. If the manure has not been early applied, it is now spread equally over the beds, and covered with earth taken from the intermediate alleys.

Mr Kelly's plan, a line is stretched along the centre of the bed, and the seed dibbled in, as already directed, along the line. This central row will be 27 inches distant from each side of the bed. After this is done, set the line 20 inches from the centre on one side, and again dibble in the seeds; and, in like manner, shift it again 20 inches on the other side of the centre row, and sow again. There would be thus three rows in each bed.'

William Kelly, in many ways, was fortunate in his employer. Sophia Evans was a charitable and agnostic Francophile who never made any unreasonable demands of his Catholic conscience. Throughout the rest of the country, many other land stewards had not been so fortunate. It is hard to know exactly how many people were evicted during the famine, as the police only began to keep an official tally in 1849. But in the five years after record keeping began, almost a quarter of a million people were recorded as being permanently evicted from their homes.

William Kelly was a Catholic. The evictees were Catholics. Catholic priests had been at the forefront of campaigns to resist evictions. So when, in October 1849, Tenant Protection Societies began to spring up in Leinster, Munster and parts of Connaught, Kelly's sympathy could almost be guaranteed. Indeed, he could hardly ignore such distress when the local workhouse at Balrothery was bursting at the seams, holding 800 inmates at the height of the famine in a facility that had only been designed for 400, and struggling to cope with another 900 people dependent on 'outdoor relief'.

Kelly's participation in direct action, however, would have to wait. For the time being, it was precluded by his employment. He was Mrs Evans' steward. His job was to ensure that the leases he offered and managed reflected the needs and wishes of his employer. He had openly and generously shared his knowledge, and few had listened. When they had, it had been to steal his ideas without thanks or attribution. Lives had been lost that could have been saved. Inevitably, it left its mark upon him.

THE GARDENERS' REVOLT

IN THE IMMEDIATE aftermath of the famine and the failed Young Ireland rebellion of 1848, the position of Irish tenant farmers and agricultural labourers had improved very little. They remained largely dependant on the potato and though the introduction of new varieties would offer some limited resistance to the *phythophtora infestans* fungus, no reliable defence would be found until the 1890s.

On the other hand, wages had risen. Almost a million had died and another million had emigrated, leaving less competition for work. The famine, ironically, had increased the bargaining power of labour and gifted higher living standards to the survivors. But with labourers in short supply and the cost of hiring them rising by the day, many landlords reacted by abandoning tillage for cattle, a far less labour intensive kind of farming.

Those labourers lucky enough to find steady work in tillage, still lived as tenants-at-will, subject to the whims of their landlords. Any improvements they made to the land still became the property of the landlord upon eviction. The Encumbered Estates Act of 1849, furthermore, now permitted creditors and bankrupts to auction off land, irrespective of who might be living upon it. Land values tumbled and hundreds of estates saddled with huge debts were auctioned off at bargain prices.

This massive sell-off attracted the attention of land speculators unsympathetic to the penniless tenants of their newly acquired investments. During the 1850s almost a quarter of the land in Ireland passed into the hands of such landlords who, anxious to create large cattle-grazing farms, raised rents and conducted mass evictions. By the 1870s, despite a worldwide economic depression, more than half of the land in the country would be in the hands of fewer than a thousand men.

Down in Portane, however, tillage remained the order of the day and, despite her advanced years, Sophia Evans' interest in farming remained as keen as ever. By now her land steward had achieved national and international fame and, at least according to the *Dublin Weekly Nation* of 16 February 1850, the raised bed system of growing green crops that he had invented was now known amongst 'all *practical* reading men' as the 'Kellyan System'. The word 'practical' had by now become less of an adjective and more of a euphemism, and antonym for the Quality.

That same year, Kelly was approached by a small group of admiring farmers who greatly valued his opinion. They asked the Portrane man if he would be willing to experiment with a new crop, one which they believed could prove immensely profitable in an Irish context. He was known to be experimenting with other crops, one more, surely, would not tax him unduly. The crop was sugar beet.

Flattered to be asked, when he had so recently and so tragically been ignored, Kelly planted a field that produced no less than twenty-six tons of tops and thirty-six tons of roots. Sugar beet had been grown commercially in continental Europe since the Napoleonic wars, but it had been slow to take off in Ireland, or indeed in Britain, where it was seen by some very powerful figures as a threat to the West Indian sugar plantations.

In producing a crop of this size, William Kelly became one of the first farmers in Ireland to grow sugar beet commercially. The results of his experiment were published in *The Farmer's Gazette* in November 1851, in the form of an open letter to the Committee of the Agricultural Museum of the Royal Dublin Society.

Kelly's crop, it should be noted, had been planted *prior* to the establishment of the Royal Irish Beet-Root Sugar Factory at Mountmellick that marked the beginnings of the Irish sugar industry. I was unable to ascertain if there was a link between the two events, but he must have been guaranteed a market for his harvest to have considered planting so much.

At the same time as Kelly was advertising the results of his sugar beet experiment, he was also selling off thirty barrels of *Victoria Bere*, a rare strain of barley. The crop had been successfully cultivated for two years on a field with a cold northerly aspect that had been 'exposed to the sea blast, and all through looked greener and hardier than wheat in the same fields'. Having proved its hardiness, and as it was the only sample of that strain at that time available in the country, Kelly placed an advertisement in *The Farmer's Gazette* offering it for sale at twenty shillings a barrel. He left samples of both the grain and straw for public inspection at the magazine's office on Dublin's Bachelor's Walk.

It says a lot about Kelly's reputation, and his relationship with Edward Purdon, that he was allowed to use the paper's office as his shop window. But

Kelly's instinct in such matters had never been about profit, and always about sharing. He very much considered himself as an agricultural scientist and wanted to be recognised as such, despite the limitations of his birth. In his desire to see intelligence transcend social class he had found an admirer, and a staunch ally, in Purdon. But it was an admiration that was not universally shared.

Courtesy of Kelly's trojan work, Sophia Evans won first prize at the RDS Agricultural Exhibition of that same year in the 'Best General and Most Extensive Collection of Farm Produce' category for no less than *thirty-six* items of prize-winning farm produce. On 23 April of the following year at the Royal Horticultural Society of Ireland Spring Show at the Rotunda Hospital, William Kelly won the prestigious Seedsman's Cup for twenty-four specimens of flowers. His victory proved unpopular amongst certain sections of the Quality.

As the summer ended Sophia Evans made an appearance at the Rathmines Horticultural Society Autumn Show. She won five prizes in various categories for her Dahlias. It was to be her last attendance at any show, of any kind. The following spring, in the company of the infamous Delia Stewart, the alleged former lover of Joseph Bonaparte, Sophia departed for France to seek expert medical care.

While she was gone, William Kelly got caught up in something of a class war within the Royal Horticultural Society of Ireland, a war he had inadvertently provoked by winning the Seedsman's Cup. There had for some time been mutterings of discontent within the lower ranks of the RHSI, where it was felt that its committees had for too long been populated by an excess of 'esquires' and a dearth of 'practical men'.

The RHSI had actually been formed by 'practical men', following a meeting held on 30 September 1816 at the Rose Tavern, in Donnybrook, when a group of estate gardeners met to share a few beers and worry about the disappearing 'art of gardening'. Resolving to exchange expertise and new ideas, they established the Horticultural Society of Ireland for gardeners who had served their time and were 'of good moral conduct'.

In the thirty-seven years since then, the society's shows and exhibitions had gained a certain social cachet and the composition of the committees had evolved to reflect that. An organisation that had once championed the work and expertise of stewards, farmers, and gardeners, had slowly become a reflection of their bondage and subservience; a socially polarised plaything for their employers.

For William Kelly, these tensions came to a head in January 1853, when he got wind of a plot to alter the rules of the RHSI to make it more difficult for the lower classes to win prestige prizes such as the Seedsman's Cup. As the current holder of the cup, Kelly was incensed and wrote to the then Secretary, James William Mackey, seeking a meeting to discuss the matter.

Under the rules of the competition, proposed and instituted back in 1851 by the competitors themselves, a meeting of the competitors was required to be called in advance of the competition to ensure that judges would be selected that were acceptable to the competitors and that a competition date would be selected that was likewise convenient for them. This hadn't happened in 1852 when William Kelly had unexpectedly won the cup, but he was determined that it *should* happen in 1853. In response to Kelly's letter, Mackey promised that he would do his best to convene a meeting.

Kelly's letter had been sent on 27 January, but Mackey's reply was not sent until 8 March. With the competition now less than a month away, Kelly, vexed beyond reason by Mackey's temporizing, fired off an angry letter demanding that a meeting take place immediately and reminding Mackey that it was incumbent upon him, as Hon. Secretary, to see to it that the rules were followed to the letter. Kelly even had the temerity, with one of his literary pike-thrusts, to accuse Mackey of having been extraordinarily lax in this regard, or perhaps even wilfully tolerant of it, in the past:

'...Now I need not tell you, that everything connected with this cup has hitherto been most irregular; but I shall take care that, if irregularity takes place on the present occasion, it shall not act to my prejudice.'

Forty-year-old James William Mackey considered himself a man of taste and refinement, entitled by birth and occupation to a place at the top table not just of the RHSI but of Dublin Society. He was not just a wealthy and well-connected seed merchant but, as the grandson of James Townsend Mackey, founder and first curator of the Trinity College Botanical Gardens, a man of impeccable horticultural pedigree.

Unlike his grandfather, however, James William Mackey was not the type of man to get his hands dirty. He employed gardeners to do that type of work. First and foremost, he was a seed merchant, and there was no better advertisement for his seeds and bulbs than his position as Secretary of the Royal Horticultural Society of Ireland. It had been a cushy little number, affording him a certain amount of stress-free prestige and free advertising ... until now.

A sybaritic individual with a taste for the flamboyant and the theatrical, Mackey was not accustomed to being called to account let alone accused of impropriety or fraud. For a young man with political aspirations, however, his terse and thin-skinned reply betrayed a worrisome lack of political artifice. Indeed, the tone of it was so utterly dismissive as to leave Kelly, who was far from a harmless or unsophisticated rustic, smarting with indignation:

Mr William Kelly.

Sir– I avail myself of the earliest leisure moment, and inform you that your communication of the 8th inst. requires no observation from me, further than to acknowledge its receipt.

I have the honour to be,
Your very humble servant,
J.W. Mackey.

Kelly rushed off an immediate and conciliatory reply. Recognising the tenor of Mackey's letter, and perhaps too the possible consequences of his uncharacteristically disproportionate umbrage, he apologised for any unintentional offence his previous letters may have caused. He had always been capable of such anger, but his outbursts, when they came, had heretofore been considered and polite. Something about Mackey, or his attitude towards him, had touched a sensitive nerve.

Hearing nothing further from Mackey, the sense of humiliation festered until Kelly could stand it no longer. He had thought himself worthy of greater respect than that; believed he had long ago surmounted his allotted station and earned the right to be counted as a gentleman. Neither time nor distance could lend reason to the dispute, nor indeed did the cessation of the epistolary exchanges serve to modify the mutual obduracy. With one choosing to be offended by a perceived lack of deference, and the other brooding on a perceived lack of respect, Mackey's silence served only to compound the insult. How else could one take it, except as an apology refused?

Determined by now to bypass the committee altogether, Kelly decided to make Mackey's treatment of his complaint a matter of public record. He would have known as he did so, as indeed would Edward Purdon, that he was making a target of himself, but paper never refused ink, and William Kelly had never backed away from a challenge. He would have respect and hang the consequences.

Whether Kelly would have been quite so gung-ho had Sophia Evans not been in France, is anybody's guess, for it was a risky strategy, on several fronts. His hard-won reputation could suffer greatly from the fall-out and his employer would hardly be gratified to discover her land steward making an enemy of the largest seed merchant in the city.

On 16 March 1853, a letter from Kelly was published in *The Farmer's Gazette* calling for a meeting of RHSI subscribers and intending competitors to take place at the offices of the Gazette on March 23rd to decide the date and place of the forthcoming exhibition and to appoint acceptable judges. Moreover, he requested that the 'Secretary to the Subscribers' attend the meeting and 'bring with him *ALL* papers connected with *ALL* former meetings on this subject'. The letter was signed 'By order of the Competitors, William Kelly'.

Even now one can scarcely avoid wincing at the use of the word 'order'. As the current holder of the Seedsman's Cup, a prize awarded for the growing of Hyacinths, Kelly claimed that he had felt compelled to act on behalf of the other competitors, few of whom seemed to have had the courage to speak up. Mackey, on the other hand, seemed intent on postponing the selection of judges and introducing a raft of restrictive new conditions, convinced that, denied the oxygen of publicity, the problem, and Kelly, would simply go away. Except, of course, they didn't.

At the meeting on 23 March, Kelly arrived primed, loaded, and ready to fire on all manner of perceived slights and inequalities. His address to the meeting, reported verbatim in the following month's *Farmer's Gazette*, could hardly have been more scathing, or embarrassing. He effectively accused the committee members of the Royal Horticultural Society of Ireland of lining their own pockets at the expense of subscribers:

'Mr Chairman, a horticultural society in any locality, but particularly the Royal Horticultural Society of Ireland, should be a most interesting, popular, and valuable institution. Such an institution, under wise management, must afford enjoyment and gratification to families who contribute the choice productions of their gardens to its exhibitions. It should afford gratification and amusement to the ladies and gentlemen within its sphere, who have not gardens themselves, by giving them an opportunity of seeing the various productions of the garden in the best condition . . .

It is to be regretted, and I regret it, that any feeling should exist tending to mar the usefulness of any institution capable of diffusing so many enjoyments and advantages. I do regret that a feeling of this kind does exist amongst gardeners generally, and I believe with justice, towards the Royal Horticultural Society. We consider that there is a spirit exhibited latterly in the proceedings of that society antagonistic to our interests. We complain of the harsh and arbitrary tendency of their published by-laws for this year, of some portion of their schedule of prizes, and of their conduct with regard to subscription prizes.

The 3rd, 4th, 5th, 10th and 12th by-laws, are nearly all new, and contain some matter slanderous to the character of gardeners generally, and altogether are arbitrary and unjust towards exhibitors.

All through these new by-laws, there is a spirit of threat towards gardeners, either directly or by implication, of "turn him out," "Expel him," "Fine him," &c., &c. I must suppose it plain enough that this is a polite way of telling the public that gardeners are generally so ill-conducted as to render these penal by-laws necessary, or that the council intended acting towards gardeners in such an unjustifiable manner as to require these by-laws to protect them.

The first of these suppositions I denounce as slanderous. Gardeners do and can conduct themselves with as much propriety - perhaps not with so much elegance - as any other class of men. The second supposition I, for one, would not submit to.

With regard to the schedule of prizes, I will confine myself to a few classes of "florists' flowers," in which amateurs are almost exclusively the exhibitors, and others in which gentlemen, or their gardeners, are the great majority of exhibitors . . . I find that for auriculas and polyanthuses, the council offered this year thirteen prizes, of the total value of £7 10s. The competitors for those prizes are only two or three, all I believe are members of the council. The prizes for hyacinths are in number fifteen, of the total value of £6 11s. The competitors are numerous, but generally gardeners.'

Kelly went on to detail other examples of questionable practices whereby the society's prize fund was weighted heavily in favour of the gentlemen members of the committee. He also highlighted the fact that new by-laws had been introduced without being proposed or seconded and were thus in breach of the society's own rules. The RHSI was being run as a private club, and he was not having it. If things did not change, he warned, it would be only too easy to fund and establish a rival horticultural society whose competitions would be based on fair play and transparency. Given the total amount of subscriptions the society collected annually from the 'practical' members, such a society was not only viable, but the RHSI would struggle to survive the split.

The meeting agreed that Kelly's complaints 'in every particular' were correct and his complaints 'just and reasonable' and agreed to meet again on 14 April to plot a course of action. To add fuel to the sense of social inequality and injustice, and just in case any of the survivors had forgotten, on 30 March the United Kingdom Census results were published showing that the population of Ireland had fallen by 1.6 million people in the last ten years. The figure was staggering, and almost all of the departed citizens had come from the same 'practical' class. It was not a good time for the upper classes to be seen to be revelling in their privileges, or taking on a man like William Kelly, who seemed to enjoy the implicit support of Edward Purdon, himself a prominent member of the RHSI.

That Purdon was quite prepared to use his magazine to support Kelly can be seen in the publication of an anonymous letter from a would-be subscriber that followed a report of Kelly's speech to the gardeners. This letter also decried the lack of 'practical men' on the committees of the Royal Horticultural Society's committees and made aspersions regarding the fairness and transparency of RHSI procedures.

Within the RHSI, wiser counsel prevailed and the executive committee refused to be drawn into a public argument. There was a time and a place for resolving such matters, and the week before the annual Spring Show was not it. Discretion was called for.

The gardeners' revolt, apart from stirring up class divisions within the RHSI had little immediate effect other than to temporarily embarrass the Honorary Secretary and, at the annual Spring Show, held at the Rotunda on 21 April, the Seedsman's Cup was won by the Earl of Charlemont. Kelly, as perhaps was to be expected after his letters to the press, failed to win a single prize in the disputed floral categories. He did, however, win first prize for his asparagus, and three days later, for his potatoes! If further words or letters were exchanged between Kelly and Mackey, they had the good grace to keep them private.

The annual general meeting of the Royal Horticultural Society of Ireland did not take place until November of that year, but when it did both Kelly and Mackey were in attendance, as indeed was Edward Purdon, whose magazine had facilitated, perhaps even encouraged the spat. Kelly's threat to set up a rival organisation was at the back of everybody's minds and, no doubt, the realisation that should he take a sizeable number of subscribers with him, the society could quickly become financially unviable. The Ascendancy enjoyed their shows and exhibitions, but very few of them were gardeners themselves.

Anxious to put the very public dispute to bed, to avoid an embarrassing scene and a damaging split in the organisation, Mackey's annual report proposed that the following year 'a very large increase in the number and value of prizes' be made available to public members, in the hope that they would continue to show their work in the society's exhibitions. Kelly had lost the battle, but he had won the war. Mackey, for his part, would learn from his mistakes, recover from the embarrassment, and go on to become Lord Mayor of Dublin and a knight of the realm.

A FRESH START

DESPITE HER HEROIC efforts to find a doctor to save her, there was nothing that could be done for Sophia Evans and she died in Paris on 24 April 1853 at the age of seventy-three. In her last will and testament, she left a gratuity of £70 to William Kelly - more than twice the amount she left to any of her other employees. All of the gratuities that Sophia Evans left to her staff were objected to by John Henry Parnell, father of Charles Stewart Parnell, who instituted legal proceedings on several fronts to delay the proving of the will.

Kelly continued to manage the Evans estate until such time as the new owner, Joshua Evans, could decide what to do with it. He had no sooner brought in his harvest, however, when Joshua's nephew, George, arrived at Portrane to run the estate as his uncle's caretaker-manager until such time as it could be sold.

Sold! That was the last thing Kelly needed to hear. He might well be kept on by the new owner, but the future was now clouded by uncertainty. He had made a home for himself in Portrane. The last thing he wanted to do was move.

The new George Evans continued to employ William Kelly as steward, but he had little interest in agriculture, and Kelly's duties were effectively reduced to that of a gardener, leaving him with excessive time on his hands. He was only forty-eight. He needed to work.

Then the war came.

Less than a year after George Evans' arrived at Portrane, Ireland fell into the grips of an unexpected and almost hysterical military enthusiasm. Young men, of all classes, rushed to enlist in the British Army to fight in a foreign war that had been precipitated by a petty dispute between France and Russia over who should control the Church of the Nativity in Bethlehem. The French supported the rights of Roman Catholics, the Russians the rights of Eastern Orthodox Christians. With Russia expanding into a Danube region then under Turkish control, Turkey and Russia went to war.

Fearful that Russia would overwhelm the Turks and push on through Afghanistan and into India, Britain and France joined the war. It was popularly assumed that the fighting would be over in months, but the fighting dragged on. With some 30,000 Irish soldiers and numerous civilians serving in the Crimea, it was followed closely at home, though not always in the manner one might expect. Not everyone wanted it to be over.

With Europe's breadbasket, southern Russia and Ukraine, cut off by the war, wheat prices once again began to rocket. A financial killing was there to be made by those willing to grasp the nettle and in no time at all the cattle barons of Meath and Kildare had ploughed their landscaped pastures in the visceral certainty that there was nothing more aesthetically pleasing than profit. It was a fortuitous time to be in tillage but, down in Portrane, there were over a hundred acres sitting idle.

It saddened those who had once depended on the Evans estate, to watch the great wheat fields become a glaucous carpet of docks and meadow grasses. The clouds of dereliction, however, paled in comparison to the shadow cast by a maritime tragedy that would leave its horrid mark upon their coastal community long after the wheat fields had been sold, even unto the present day.

In January 1854, the RMS Tayleur set sail from Liverpool on her maiden voyage to Melbourne carrying six-hundred souls to the antipodean gold rush. She was a 230ft full-rigged iron clipper, bigger and, allegedly, safer than any vessel of her kind. The pride of the White Star Line, she was manned by an experienced captain, a largely inexperienced crew, and navigated by means of a compass that had never been adequately tested on an iron-hulled ship. On the night of 21 January, she got lost in heavy fog and stormy seas and ran aground off Seal Hole Bay on the east side of Lambay Island, just two miles off Portrane.

Of the six hundred souls on board, three hundred and sixty drowned, the vast majority of them women and children. The behaviour of desperate passengers and crew shocked Victorian Britain and the loss of national virtue was mourned almost as sorrowfully as the loss of life. For a few weeks, the words *courage* and *chivalry* seemed almost lost to the English language or, at the very least, were redefined as actions independent of race.

For the people of Portrane, the disaster lasted far longer than a single night or a couple of weeks of journalistic soul-searching. Bodies continued to wash ashore for months and because of the lack of religious identification, many were refused full burial rights by Catholic and Protestant clergy alike. It probably didn't help that many of the crew had been Indian and Chinese.

Of the bloated corpses that washed ashore at Portrane, some were buried by estate workers at Knocknaman (the highest point in The Burrow) and others at The Stranger's Bank. For a population that had only recently survived the ravages of the Great Famine, it was a timely reminder of the fickleness of fate.

A little over a year later, as they approached their twentieth wedding anniversary, William and Mary Jane decided to take perhaps the greatest risk of their lives. William needed to work, but the Evans estate no longer demanded so much of his time. He could have started again as a steward someplace else, but Portrane was now home. He could not bring himself to leave.

Rather than watch the land that he had so diligently cultivated for over a decade, and for which he had developed a proprietorial affection, be allowed to go completely wild, William decided to lease over a hundred acres from George Evans and farm it for his own benefit. It was a romantic notion, after all these years, to finally have his own farm, but the decision was neither impulsive nor naïve. Since the end of the famine, in 1851, food prices had been rising rapidly and, with the Crimean war still raging, there was real money to be made in tillage. If Evans wasn't prepared to do it, then Kelly was more than willing to do so.

The lease was for a period of twenty-one years, by which time, if still living, William would be seventy years of age and Mary Jane seventy-nine. Never a man for making crazed decisions, Kelly had carefully weighed and measured the various merits and demerits of the gamble and judged the risk acceptable. But it was still a risk and Nature, as they knew only too well by now, could be a fickle mistress.

The Kellys acquired fields in the townlands of Ballymastone, Ballalease South, and of course at Middlefield, where William decided to build a new two-story Georgian farmhouse for himself and Mary Jane in keeping with their new status. The house would be built onto the gable end of the existing cottage with a south-facing frontage.

The same care and attention to detail that Kelly applied to his agricultural methodology now went into the design of his new home. The house was constructed facing so exactly south that, on the day of the winter solstice, the sun would shine through the clear glass fanlight above the hall door to illuminate the back wall of the kitchen. It does this to this day, on the day of the winter solstice, and on no other day of the year.

By incorporating the cottage rather than demolishing and re-building, Kelly not only indulged his passion for recycling, he ensured that he and Mary Jane would always have a reminder of the life they were leaving behind, and to which they could so easily return. He would also build stables, offices, barns, sheds, and a coach house for the farm (many of which, like the house itself, are still standing today). Crucially, whether by accident or design, the lease was drafted without any reservation of the exclusive right of the landlord to game.

From Middlefield, Kelly could no longer see the outline of the Wicklow mountains as he worked, or enjoy the sense of being by the sea, but the kestrels still fluttered above the fields in the mornings, the seagulls still followed the plough and, on windless spring days, the cuckoos could still be heard in the woods of Mount Evans. The cliffs were still just a half hour's walk away, should they ever need to take the sea air, but there would be little time for leisure now as they had an ambitiously large enterprise to manage. They would need to be a team: different accents, but a single voice. To stand still was to go backwards, or to rot.

Middlefield c.1975. Photo courtesy of Gordon Henderson.

At the time Kelly took out his lease with George Evans, many of his friends and neighbours, particularly those leasing large farms, had become involved with the Tenant Right League, a predominantly middle-class organization established in 1850 with the aim of reforming the Irish land system. Founded by Charles Gavan Duffy and Frederick Lucas, it had initially enjoyed the support of both Protestant and Catholic tenants and, in particular, of a progressive young farmer from Malahide called Andrew Kettle, with whom Kelly had become quite friendly.

The league had sought to secure the adoption and enforcement of the Three Fs, namely: Fair Rent, Fixity of Tenure, and Free Sale, with fair rent being the priority of small farmers, and fixity of tenure the priority of larger farmers like Kettle. They enjoyed some initial political success, fifty candidates being elected to parliament in the general election of 1852, but the Catholic members soon formed a breakaway movement, the Catholic Defence Association (a.k.a. The Pope's Brass Band) and the movement fragmented.

Outraged at the introduction of sectarian motives into the land struggle, Frederick Lucas took his increasingly indignant protests about the powerful Archbishop of Dublin, Paul Cullen, to Rome and promptly lost the support of the Catholic clergy. Lucas died a broken man in October 1855. The following month Gavan Duffy emigrated to Australia, where he became Prime Minister of the state of Victoria. The outbreak of the Crimean war and the rapid rise in agricultural prices had since put a halt to the gallop of the tenants' rights movement. Farmers were simply too busy to rock the boat.

Kelly had been very much supportive of the Tenant Right League, but he'd had little time to spare for active engagement in politics. Having just leased more than one hundred acres from George Evans, he was now under pressure to make it pay. He had also, by degrees, begun to take over the leases of other tenants who had decided, for one reason or another, to surrender them. By the time he had finished, he had amassed one hundred and sixty acres.

Much as had been the case when he first arrived at Portrane, Kelly's first task involved the reclamation of waterlogged or badly farmed land and the repair of some of the labourers' cottages that had been neglected since Sophia Evans' death. To keep his landlord sweet, he had also continued to maintain the lawns and gardens of Portrane House. He was, once again, a busy man.

Things were changing rapidly in Ireland, and not just politically. The industrial revolution had seen the invention of farming machines. This was bad news for the farm labourers that just a decade previous had been so vital to Kelly's methods of farming. Not all of them were content to stand idly by. In March of 1859, Kelly was called to give evidence to an inquiry, the funding for which he had personally contributed the sum of £5. He had done so in concert with other Catholic farmers of the peninsula anxious to remove any suggestion of a revival of Ribbonism amongst the Catholics of the district. The last thing they needed at that time was agrarian agitation or official intervention.

The inquiry had been provoked by a series of arson attacks on the properties of a Mr John Mills, a Protestant farmer from Corballis, in Donabate. The first took place at his haggard, on 19 November 1858, during which a large amount of his property as well as his store of wheat and oats were destroyed. The second occurred at the same location on 6 March 1859, and the third four days later at a row of cabins inhabited by his tenants.

Rumours had circulated that the fires had been started maliciously by Catholic labourers: the wagging tongues prompted by the anti-Catholic views of Mills' wife, who had allegedly named her pig 'Father McCarthy', after the Catholic parish priest. Mills himself was said to be a good landlord, if not a great farmer, and to have got on well with his Catholic workers. Though it was suggested by some that all three fires could have been accidentally set by his pipe-smoking brother, the most likely scenarios were an act of malice by a disgruntled labourer or an act of insurance fraud by Mills himself (local rumours had placed his father-in-law at the scene of the first fire and he was known to be struggling financially).

According to Mills, he had recently chastised some labourers and threatened to replace them with a type of machine similar to that which William Kelly was now using on his own lands: 'I had a dispute in this way with the men that got in my harvest; I found fault with the way they reaped, and said, I am so far independent of them as I could get the reaping done by the machine; they laughed and said I would not do so.' In the end, the inquiry found that the fires had been started maliciously, but no arrests were ever made.

Despite the suggestion of vengeance by a disgruntled labourer over Mills' threat to use a machine to bring in the harvest, Kelly, with a constant eye on farm economy, had not been slow in embracing new technological advances. For so long his methods had relied on cheap labour, but that was no longer available.

In July 1859, an article in *The Freeman's Journal* reported that the man who had once been so reluctant to plough with horses had been spotted on Portrane Demesne using a machine, newly invented by Burgess and Hayes of London, that was capable of both mowing *and* reaping. The previous month he had been a judge in the 'horticultural implements' category of the RDS Horticultural Exhibition. The world was changing. You could not simply turn your back on it.

THE MARY JANES OF MIDDLEFIELD

MARY JANE, MARY Jane, Mary Jane. What was it about that name that caused it to be so ubiquitous amongst the Shanks family? Amongst Mary Jane Kelly's close relatives there were at least three more, two of whom were about to join her at Middlefield House.

On 22 January 1860, Mary Jane Kelly's brother, James Shanks, died at his rented dwelling on 65 Lower Mecklenburg Street, Dublin. He was just sixty-three years of age. His death was announced with a modest three-line notice in the Dublin evening papers:

'January 20, at 65, Lower Mecklenburgh Street, Mr James Shanks, much and deservedly regretted by all who knew him. May he rest in peace.'

James was buried in Prospect Cemetery, Glasnevin, in a grave purchased for him by William Kelly. Unusually, the grave already contained a body, that of a Francis Neill, of Mark Street (off Pearse Street) in Dublin's south inner city. Neill had died in 1848, at the age of 70. While not entirely beyond the realms of possibility, there is little to suggest a relationship with the Shanks family.

James Shanks' daughter, unmarried twenty-five-year-old Mary Jane Shanks, and her 'adopted' twenty-two-year-old 'sister', Mary Jane Derrick, had for some time been entirely dependent on the sixty-three-year-old widower. But now, with James gone, there was no one left to support them and, with nowhere else to go, they cleared the flat of everything of value and came to live with the Kellys at Middlefield. It was either that, the workhouse, or the brothel.

At the time of his death, James Shanks had been living as a tenant in a building owned by acting inspector of police, Thomas Grattan. We can probably assume, therefore, that the tenants were reputable. The street itself, however, had an entirely different reputation. The area was a slum and rents were low. It was situated close to Amiens Street train station, Dublin Port, and Aldborough Barracks – prime real estate for prostitutes.

In Dublin, at this time, there were more than a hundred and thirty unofficially tolerated brothels operating openly in the city, the majority of them situated in the tenement buildings that lay between Montgomery Street and Lower Mecklenburg Street. Known colloquially as 'Monto', the area was well on its way to becoming the largest red-light district in Europe.

Many of the tenement buildings on Lower Mecklenburg Street were home to famous madams and housed brothels that operated cheek by jowl with the local Magdalen Asylum, opened by the sisters of Charity in 1822. Pregnant women, abandoned to care for themselves, were a common sight on the street and their children, known locally as 'Monto babies', were often 'adopted' by kind-hearted locals.

In 1880 brothels would be recorded as operating quite openly at numbers 20, 39, 82-85, and 104-105 Lower Mecklenburgh Street, but there had been brothels on the street since at least the latter half of the previous century, the most famous of them being run by Mrs Mary (Moll) Hall, a close friend of the infamous Margaret Leeson. It was not the best place for a respectable working-class woman to find herself with no steady income, or indeed two respectable women for that matter.

It is not known exactly what the relationship between James Shanks and May Derrick was, but it must have been close, for when Michael and 'May' Derrick died, James had taken in their nine-year-old daughter and raised her as his own. When James himself died, therefore, it wasn't just his twenty-five-year-old daughter Mary Jane Shanks, that was left without a home or means of support, Mary Jane Derrick was also, and for the third time in her life, left similarly bereft. They had thus far avoided the seedier aspects of life in 'Monto', but what was to become of them now?

With nowhere else to go the two Mary Janes, who had effectively been raised as sisters, had little option now but to accept Mary Jane Kelly's offer of home at Middlefield. Whatever issues had caused their parents' estrangement from Mary Jane Kelly, they had to be put aside now. The transition would be dramatic. T'was far from trees and meadows *they'd* been raised.

The farmhouse at Middlefield sat on a windy hilltop with its face to the prevailing wind. In winter the rain could drive so ferociously against the bedroom windows as to rattle them in their boxes. Unlike in the city, there were no tall buildings to muffle its roar. You woke on a winter's morning fully conscious of what the weather was doing outside.

On calmer days, when the sun showed its smiling face, you wiped the morning's condensation from the pane to reveal a knotted carpet of fields and hedgerows that stretched all the way to the woods at Mount Evans. Occasionally, rabbits would bob across the drive and kestrels would flutter in the sky: on Lower Mecklenburgh Street it had been pigeons and rats.

Whenever they had needed to escape the cramped confines of their Mecklenburg Street flat, the two Mary Janes had always been able to walk to the Phoenix Park or St. Stephen's Green. But it was another matter entirely to be able to stroll through a landscape like this. Here a young woman could take a lone walk to the village shop without being propositioned by drunks or taunted by prostitutes. At Middlefield only the trees loitered in lanes and, as they stretched out before them, the fields themselves seemed to throw a protective arm around them and push that darker world away. And if ever they needed reminding of the breadth of the social chasm they had just crossed, they need look no further than the servants' bell in their bedroom.

But why now and not earlier? Why had James Shanks not sought the Kellys' help when the girls were younger. They could just as easily have moved to Middlefield in their early teens and avoided having to grow up on a street where prostitution had been all but normalised. The prostitutes and madams, after all, were their neighbours. They walked the same streets, drank in the same bars, and bought in the same shops. They were, as much as many would have wished it otherwise, very much a part of their tightly knit community.

If the Kellys were willing to take in the girls now to save them from a life of destitution or worse, it seems likely that they would also have been willing to take them sooner. Whatever the reason for the delay, it ran deep, and the girls had probably been raised with only one side of it. But that was not going to get in Mary Jane Kelly's way now. The girls were coming to Middlefield and that was that. They could not possibly be left to fend for themselves in the heart of 'Monto'. The Shanks were not that kind of family.

Middlefield c.1961. Photo courtesy of Gordon Henderson

The moil and toil of life on a farm would have taken some getting used to. There could be no passengers on such an enterprise, and no escaping the expectation that they would learn the chores of a farmer's daughter and diligently earn their keep like every other working member of the household. There were servants, of course, to help with the heavier tasks, but there were also the lighter chores of the farm to be shared, and strange smells to become accustomed to, smells that often offended the olfactory senses of city people.

In time the girls would also need new clothes, or shoes, or something else that they would have to ask for, and that would perhaps also be a difficult bridge to cross, the solicitation of charity always being hardest that first time. But they could not go on as they once had, they had climbed the social ladder and would now need to dress in a manner that reflected the social status of the household. They would also have to accustom themselves to both the presence and function of servants. It was a lot to take in and though they were doubtlessly thankful, that type of gratitude can be exhausting.

But it wasn't just the girls that needed to adjust, for having so long resigned themselves to never having a family of their own, the Kellys' domestic routines suddenly had to accommodate the discomfiture of two virtual strangers. A household of four people would, by necessity, behave in a very different manner to a household of two.

All of a sudden there were two more voices in the house, two more chairs placed around the sitting room fire, two more places to be set at the dinner table, and two more mouths to feed. The floorboards now creaked in what used to be the spare bedroom and items of unfamiliar clothing began to be draped over the backs of chairs.

Saturday baths would now take forever, and water would now have to be shared. The washing of clothes would similarly take twice the time and other, long-established, domestic routines would have to be torn asunder and rewritten. Frustration was inevitable. Time, patience, and understanding, would be needed. On all sides.

The upheaval had been forced upon the Kellys, but if it had to be borne with fortitude, it had also, perhaps, to be welcomed with gratitude. It was never going to be anything but difficult, but perhaps the sound of youthful laughter about the house made it all worthwhile. If the extra noise and constant chatter occasionally drove William to the farmyard office to finish work that he might once have taken care of at the dining room table, then perhaps that, too, was a price worth paying. William was fifty-four, his wife was sixty-three. This was as close as either of them had, or ever would come, to having children of their own. They could, at long last, claim to have a family.

BALROTHERY POOR LAW UNION

Remains of the Chapel – Balrothery Union Workhouse at Lusk

THE IRISH POOR Law Act of 1838 had divided the country into one hundred and thirty poor law unions each with a workhouse at its centre. These unions, the precursors of today's County Councils and Health Boards, dealt primarily with matters of destitution, public safety, and public health. They were run by boards of guardians which, since 1847, had been comprised of two types of members: elected members, who comprised one half of the board, and ex-officio members, who held their positions by virtue of their status in the local community e.g. magistrates and large landowners.

The work of the guardians was funded by the Poor Rate, which the guardians were empowered to levy in their union districts. As most of the guardians were large property owners themselves, they were effectively setting the rate of their own taxes, with all that that implied for the financing of those institutions that relied on them. In the years since the famine, a significant drop in the population had seen less demand for Poor Law services, and Poor Rates had fallen nationally. No guardian wanted to see them increased.

The Fingal area of north County Dublin was catered for by the Balrothery Poor Law Union. It covered an area of approximately 120 square miles in which, at the outset of the famine, there had resided more than 280,000 people. It ran six medical dispensaries and the odd primary school. It also ran the fever hospital and workhouse at Lusk.

At its famine peak, this workhouse had catered for almost eight hundred residents; twice its official capacity. Over the course of the 1850s, these responsibilities were expanded further to include the 'boarding out' of children, which involved the placing of poor children in long-term foster care and the payment of an allowance to the foster parents who cared for them. In their essence, then, the Poor Law Unions represented an early form of state-funded social welfare and the guardians that ran them something of a civil/political hybrid who laboured under the legal supervision of the Poor Law Commissioners.

Any local man who held property with a rateable valuation of greater than £4 was entitled to vote in the election of guardians. But not all property owners were equal. The balance of power was weighted in favour of the large landowners. If a man's property was valued at greater than £200, then it was possible that he would be entitled to as many as six votes, the number being determined on a graduated scale.

With the passing of the Medical Charities (Ireland) Act in 1851, the poor law guardians were allowed to divide their unions into dispensary districts, each of which would maintain a dispensary and provide medical assistance to the poor. The unions would fund the stocking of the dispensaries and pay the salaries of the, largely part-time, medical officers and their assistants, effectively providing the first type of community medicine that was widely available in Ireland.

In July 1852, while he was still working for Sophia Evans, whose health was failing rapidly, William Kelly had applied to the Balrothery Poor Law Union to have his property rated, suggesting that he had by that time been allowed to purchase the cottage in which he had lived for so long. The Balrothery guardians' minute book recorded the request, but also the fact that a decision on the rateable valuation had been postponed for further enquiry, suggesting, perhaps, that the cottage and land may not have merited an obvious rateable value above the minimum.

Five years later, however, following the death of Sophia Evans and Kelly's lease of 160 acres to farm in his own right, not to mention his building of a two-storey Georgian house onto the pre-existing cottage, he tried again, and, on 20 August 1857, the board finally approved his request. William Kelly had become a 'substantial farmer' and, more importantly, an eligible voter.

But not only did Kelly become eligible to vote in his own right, he also became eligible to act as a proxy voter for other landowners, which he did on several occasions. One of the men for whom he acted as a proxy, in February 1858, was Joshua Evans, the brother-in-law of his late employer, Sophia Evans, and his current landlord. It spoke volumes for the esteem in which he was held, both as a tenant and as a man, and indeed for the harmonious state of his relationship with the Evans family.

So great was this esteem, and the fame that had followed his efforts to modernise the outlook and practices of Irish farmers during the famine that, in August 1856, *The Farmer's Gazette* sent a journalist to Donabate to interview him. It is possible, perhaps even probable, that this anonymous journalist was none other than Edward Purdon himself, joint owner of the *Gazette.*

At the time of this visit, Kelly had recently taken in hand a 'worn-out farm' immediately adjoining Portrane Demesne with a view to improving it for a future tenant. The land on which this farm sat had been thoroughly cleared and sown with a Hungarian variety of black oats that Kelly had sourced from the Lord Mayor of Dublin, Joseph Boyce. The farm was not identified.

When walking the journalist through a turnip field, Kelly proceeded to identify a patch where the sown crop appeared to be far superior to the rest of the field. This patch, Kelly informed his interviewer, had been sown by means of the dibble, the drill machine having been stopped in its tracks by heavy rain on the day in question. So skilfully had the patch been sown that there were no gaps.

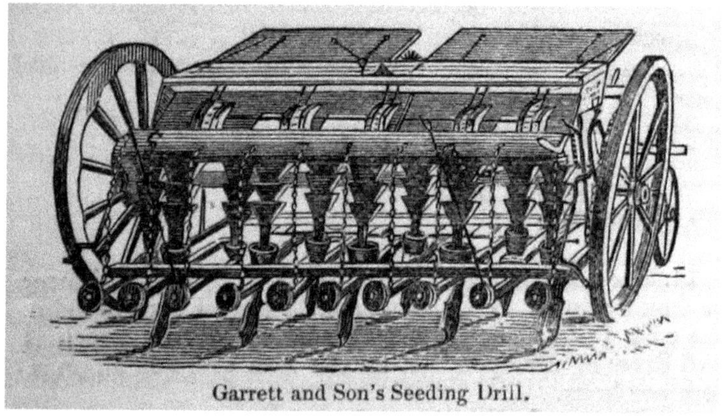
Garrett and Son's Seeding Drill.

Image courtesy of Grace's Guide to British Industrial History

Given his methods of farming during the famine when labourers' wages were low, it would have come as no surprise to find that Kelly had retreated to the use of the dibble, but Kelly was no Luddite. In fact, Kelly had not only been one of the first farmers in Ireland to use a mowing and reaping machine, he had also been the first Irish farmer to trial Garret's Drill Machine, the first to adopt it, and the first to advocate its use.

This article, published on 6 August 1856 in *The Farmer's Gazette*, gives us some idea of the influence Kelly had exerted on Irish farming during the previous decade. Written just five years after the end of the Great Famine, when the memory of that catastrophe was still fresh in the minds of all who had lived through it, it marks a significant recognition of his place in the history of the period. One paragraph in particular warrants special notice:

'Any one who calls at the Donabate station, and having an hour or two to spare, will miss a source of much gratification if he omits visiting Portrane, which has been so long under the managing care of our old friend Mr William Kelly. We have often regretted that Mr Kelly has for some years refrained from mixing publicly in agricultural discussions; for there are assuredly few better adapted for being a clear and sound expositor of the principle and practice of the science. At one time the case was different, and when Ireland required all the energies which could be called into action, in order to raise the country from that state of almost hopeless prostration into which it had sunk, Mr Kelly did not hesitate to step forward and lend his powerful aid in the great work of re-invigoration. He who writes the history of Ireland's social condition and progress, during the dark days to which we refer, will leave his task unfinished if he omits from his pages the name of William Kelly.'

Had it been written a quarter of a century later, it might have served as a fitting obituary. However, despite the fact that the man who penned this piece was in all probability still alive when Kelly died, and the fact that by then he would have been a former Lord Mayor of Dublin, there would never be any published obituary for William Kelly.

All that lay in the future. For the time being, William Kelly was just a highly intelligent tenant farmer with a finely-tuned moral compass and a natural empathy for the poor and downtrodden. He had a voice now, and a vote in his own right. And he was determined to use it. Having been silent for so long on matters agricultural, Kelly was now about to raise his head in the political arena, and on a controversial matter on which he was something of an expert – manure!

THE ROGERSTOWN EMBANKMENT AFFAIR

Embankment at Rogerstown Estuary

ON THE EVENING of 28 November 1861, the *Evening Freeman* carried a notice of intention, from unnamed individuals, to apply for an Act of Parliament to incorporate a commercial company, the sole object of which was to effect the embankment and reclamation of land within the Rogerstown Estuary.

William Kelly had never been a man to oppose the reclamation of wasteland, if it was truly waste. Indeed, he had done so several times on the Evans Estate himself. But, with its narrow and shallow estuary and its extensive seaweed-covered mudflats, Rogerstown represented a special case.

The lands surrounding the Rogerstown Estuary were home to over eight hundred families, the majority of whom eked out a meagre living on smallholdings of sandy soil that for centuries had been fertilised by a freely collectable seaweed known locally as 'woar' (bladderwrack). A similar tradition had long existed at Bannow. But there the collection of seaweed had been restricted to the tenants of Thomas Boyse, landlord of the Bannow Farm School. Used primarily as fertiliser, the availability of seaweed was considered so valuable to farmers that rents for coastal holdings around Bannow Bay were often higher than those inland. A single cartload was worth the equivalent of a week's wage for a farm labourer.

A similar situation had also long existed on the Malahide Estuary. In the decade prior to the famine, prosecutions for the large-scale theft of seaweed from the shores at Kilcrea and Corballis by convoys of raiders from the Rush side of the Rogerstown estuary had been common. The shoreline here was owned by the Cobbe family, who had similarly attempted to protect their rights to it at significant financial cost. No such impediment, however, had ever been imposed around the Rogerstown Estuary.

Seaweed was considered especially suitable for the fertilisation of root crops such as potatoes, turnips, and mangelwurzel. Indeed, without it, the poor land around the estuary would quickly become unsuitable for tillage. Potatoes, still the staple of the pauper's diet, were *especially* fond of seaweed and some varieties were even known to be capable of growing in piles of seaweed alone. On poor land, it had become an almost traditional remedy to use a mixture of seaweed, sand,

and manure to strengthen the soil. In fact, in the Burrow of Portrane, the mixture of sandy soil and seaweed fertiliser had in the past afforded the area an unusual degree of protection from blight.

Bladderwrack Seaweed

The sandy soil that surrounded the Rogerstown estuary was difficult to farm. Cattle manure alone was next to useless on it except when mixed with seaweed and ploughed into the soil. The seaweed provided a balanced source of trace elements, growth hormones, nutrients, and disease preventatives, the actions of which to this day are still not fully understood. Without the seaweed, the small farmers of the estuary would have been unable to afford other, more expensive, forms of fertilizer and would consequently have been unable to grow sufficient crops to feed their families. Ultimately, they would have been forced to abandon their farms.

The consequences for the community at large, Kelly predicted, would be catastrophic. Unable to farm the land, the smallholders would be unable to pay their rents or feed themselves. They would swiftly find themselves crouched in supplication on the steps of the Balrothery Workhouse, which although no longer overcrowded was still catering for over two hundred inmates, i.e. approximately half its maximum capacity. It would be incapable of accepting even a half of the numbers who could find themselves displaced as a result of reclamation.

Amongst those families likely to be affected was the family of Kelly's good friend, William Nolan, who lived with his five children on a small farm at Nethercross, in The Burrow. Nolan and Kelly had become so close in recent years that Nolan had made Kelly one of the executors of his will, and a potential guardian of his youngest children. That made the issue more than a moral one, it made it personal.

Considered an expert by now on all things agricultural, even by the large landowners of the county, Kelly knew his opinion on certain matters would carry weight locally, but little influence where it mattered most, in Westminster. But there was little point in raging in impotent fury, he needed to cultivate allies to stop the project in its tracks, allies like the influential lords and men of eminence that comprised the Board of Guardians of the Balrothery Poor Law Union.

On 18 December 1861, despite the fact that speculative land deals were not really within their remit, William Kelly wrote a strongly worded letter to the Balrothery guardians regarding the proposed land reclamation works at the slobs of the Rogerstown estuary. In his letter, he attempted to undermine the financial credibility of the project and to detail 'the great injury to the poor that will result' should the project be allowed to go ahead. He called upon the guardians to join him in opposing the proposed reclamation.

Kelly's letter was received the following day and scheduled to be read to the Board of Guardians at their next meeting on 8 January 1862. Despite the seriousness of the situation, this was the only letter of protest on this subject that the board would receive. By the time they met, however, the board would be already familiar with the contents of the letter, primarily because Kelly was not about to allow them to ignore it, or indeed him.

Six days prior to sending his letter to the Board of Guardians, Kelly had written a similar letter, on 12 December 1861, to the *Farmer's Gazette*, to which he had continued to a be regular contributor over the years. Laden with sardonic prose, and seething with moral outrage, it was published on 21 December 1861, just enough in advance of the Board of Guardians meeting as to apply substantial public pressure.

THE ROGERSTOWN RECLAMATION AND EMBANKMENT COMPANY

SIR, - About the 20th of November, ultimo, I received, through the Post office, a printed paper purporting to be the prospectus of the "Rogerstown Reclamation and Embankment Company," with a printed "form of application for shares." I believe this is the usual course with joint stock companies in soliciting parties to take shares in their company. In this prospectus there was no list of directors or managers, as is usual in such cases; and in the printed form of application for shares it is requested that the document be returned to the "Provisional Committee of the Rogerstown Reclamation and Embankment Company, and William H. Johnson Esq., Honorary Secretary, 53, Lower Dominick Street, Dublin.

I am intimately acquainted with the "Rogerstown strand," and I have taken some trouble to satisfy myself whether it would be a safe investment to take shares in this professed company; for it appears to me that, as yet, there is no real company, else why "the provisional committee." I have examined the project as the speculation of enterprising individuals, and as the conception of some philanthropists, and I have from the facts that presented themselves arrived at the conclusions following: –

The "Provisional Committee" states – 1st. That the land to be reclaimed will form an area of about 700 acres (I presume statute acres); 2nd. That when reclaimed, they will set or sell this land to the best advantage; 3rd. That the work and all expenses will be covered by a sum of £12,000.

From my knowledge of the Rogerstown estuary I know that there is a considerable portion adjoining the lands of Portrane that, if well reclaimed, would make very good land. The same applies to a great proportion of the slob west of the railway, and there is some deep, heavy land on a small portion east of the railway bridge; but from Rogerstown harbour to the Lugford, on both sides of the river, and from the Lugford to the western ford on to the Raheen point, north of the river, with the margin between the clayland and the bed of the estuary all round, averaging in depth about twenty yards, the whole consisting of about one-half the area of the entire estuary, is composed of as bad materials for land as ever a crow flew over. To a great extent the soil is bare – a brick clay, as hard as dried putty, and as tough as wax; in other parts this obdurate brick clay is covered with a mixture of itself and gravel, forming a perfect grout; and in other parts it is covered with a hungry blowing sand.

Supposing, therefore, the entire estuary was rendered dry on the surface, I would value one-half of it at 20s per acre (32s per Irish acre), and the other half at 6s 8d per acre (10s 8d per Irish acre). This valuation would bring a gross rental yearly of £466 13s 4d., which, if divided amongst the shareholders, would give them 3 ½ per cent. on their capital and leave £46 13s 4d to meet the income tax and poor-rate collectors, and nothing at all for agency or management. If, however, the directors sold the entire lot, and got twenty-five years' purchase, they would have £11,666 13s 4d., or £333 6s 8d less than the shareholders subscribed, or, in other words, a loss to that amount. It is evident, therefore, that as a private speculation, this reclamation concern will be a losing concern; and my conclusion is – I shall take no shares.

But, again, viewing this company as practical philanthropists, what can they effect by this reclamation scheme? Of course, they will in effecting the works necessarily give a large amount of labour, or employment, not much required in this district; but some parties requiring employment would get it, and it would effect a public good to that amount. The produce of the land when reclaimed would add to the available food of the country in the shape of potatoes, oats, beef, milk, and butter, to the amount of the quantity of such articles extracted from the land. These are the good things that could be effected. Let us consider all the evils that would be effected at the same time.

The townland of the Burrow contains 262a. 3r. 5p. occupied by 49 families; the townland of Rush contains 1,171a. 2r. 26p., upon which there are 767 families, occupying from less than 1 rood to 4 acres each. Now, the whole of the soil of the Burrow, and nearly all of these smallholdings in Rush, is almost a pure sand or a loamy sand; and it is well known that no amount of farmyard manure will produce crops in this sandy soil without the addition of seaweed.

Now, these 816 families produced excellent crops of potatoes, carrots, some good wheat, and clover and ray grass off these 1,434a. 1r. 31p. of land, almost wholly by the application of seaweed, which they got to a great extent off this estuary about being reclaimed; which, when done, these 1,434 acres will, to a great extent, go out of cultivation, and many of the 816 families, I fear, to the poorhouse. The injury, in a public view, will also be very great, because the potato crop in these sandy lands has always escaped the disease and contributed a large share to the Dublin market as well as for export to Wales.

But this is not all. The harbour of Rogerstown will be destroyed by this reclamation. At this harbour there has been annually sold 4,000 tons of coals, which after the embankment must be got from Malahide, or Balbriggan, or Skerries; the difference of the cost of cartage alone to the parishioners of Rush, Lusk, Donabate, and Portrane will be about 2s per ton, or a loss to the sellers of about £100. There are also 120 sailors in the town of Rush engaged in the coal trade of the harbour of Rogerstown and in fishing. After the reclamation these sailors, with their families, will be in the position of Othello – their occupation will be gone.

Again, there are at least 100 women from Lusk, Rush, and Donabate who make a livelihood every year, or the greater part of every year, by gathering shellfish on this estuary; some of their husbands or fathers earn money by driving these shellfish to Dublin market. After the reclamation, this earning is all gone, and this class, or these women, must go to the workhouse.

Again, the little children and girls earned something by catching "winkles" to feed their ducks, which after the reclamation they can do no more. But, last of all, and worst of all, 52 acres of the lands adjoining are sought to enable these philanthropists to effect their reclamation, with the houses, offices, haggards, and gardens of some of the very best of inhabitants.

Thus, for the apocryphal good which these speculators or philanthropists may effect, they will, most certainly, destroy 816 families; put to a great extent out of cultivation 1,434 acres, 1 rood 31 perches of land; mulct the parishioners of Rush, Lusk, Donabate, and Portrane in the buying of their coals and selling of their potatoes to the amount of £500 annually, destroy the business of 120 fishermen and sailors, and thereby ruin their families; drive to the poorhouse 100 women, shell fish gatherers; destroy the prospects of even the little children, and exterminate some of the most respectable and industrious families to be found, of their class, in any country.

I believe I am correct in the above statement, but there is one additional item which they will accomplish – they will diminish the rents of those grounds to the landlords to a very great extent, indeed.

I must suppose that the promoters of this scheme were not, nor are not, aware of all the injury they would impose on the poor people, and I hope when they are aware of it, they will desist in their design.

Yours &c.,
Wm. Kelly,
Portrane,
Donabate,
December 12, 1861.

Two days before the scheduled meeting of the Balrothery Poor Law Union Board of Guardians, in January 1862, a public meeting was held at the schoolhouse in Rush to rally opposition to the proposed reclamation. In attendance were many of the Balrothery guardians and most of the local landlords. William Kelly's arguments and figures were repeated almost verbatim, but Kelly was neither reported as being in attendance, nor were his arguments or figures credited when the meeting was reported on the front page of the *Evening Freeman* of 11 January.

At a Board of Guardians meeting two days later, due regard *was* given to Kelly's letter, and it is clearly identified as the source of the subsequent resolution, but no thanks or recognition were offered for bringing the matter to their attention. Despite the advent of Catholic emancipation, it seemed, background remained important. Kelly's letters, nevertheless, had had the desired effect. They had prompted a separate but significant realisation that was all the more powerful for its appeal to naked self-interest.

With the expected hordes descending upon the workhouse for relief, not only would the landowners of the board lose rents on poor land, they would face a significant increase in their poor rates. Well, they were not having that.

Unanimously, they resolved that:

'… having examined the map and prospectus of the intended embankment and enclosure of Rogerstown Slob Lands, we, whilst disclaiming any intention of interfering with matters which do not come within our province as Guardians of the Poor and Representatives of the Ratepayers, feel sound to oppose by every legitimate means in our power this proposed encroachment on the sustenance of over 500 families; for should this speculation be carried out, it will be the means of creating a large amount of pauperism within the Union, which must be met by an increased assessment of poor rates to maintain a large number of smallholders of land in the neighbourhood of Rush and the Borough of Donabate, who will be unable to support themselves out of the workhouse if they be deprived of the seaweed periodically deposited on the Rogerstown estuary, and which from time immemorial they have had the privilege of using in the cultivation of the sandy soil of which their several holdings are composed, farm yard manure being unsuited for the purpose unless aided by seaweed.

Resolved unanimously that in the event of any bill being presented to parliament to carry out this project, we will petition against it, and likewise memorial the Lords of the Admiralty, praying them to withhold their sanction and give opposition to the proposed enclosure of those lands.'

The resolution was published in the *Irish Times* and *Freeman's Journal* of the following Saturday. But once again, Kelly's name was not mentioned. His arguments and figures (slightly reduced, as though the Board of Guardians was reluctant to appear alarmist) *were* mentioned but, again, the source was unattributed.

Locally, however, everybody would have known of Kelly's very public intervention. Natural disasters have a habit of bonding a community together, and Kelly had lived through two of the worst with his friends and neighbours in the hurricane of 1839 and the famine of 1845. He might once have been considered a 'blow-in' to Portrane, but the community had long since taken him into their lives and he was very much part of the fabric of it now. Furthermore, the majority of local farmers would have read *The Farmer's Gazette* and known that it was Kelly who had struck first.

Something else that may have been recognised locally was the unspoken threat that if the farmers of the Rogerstown Estuary could not get their seaweed at Rogerstown, they would, before resigning themselves to the workhouse, go elsewhere in search of it, leading to a potential resumption of the 'seaweed wars' that had blighted the Malahide Estuary in the decade before the famine.

On 7 February, the Freeman's Journal reported that the 'Rogerstown Embankment and Reclamation Bill had passed the examining barrister of the House of Commons. A report on the matter, however, had still to be received from the Admiralty, who were obliged under the Preliminary Enquiries Act, to investigate the proposal. The Admiralty were stalling. They had received influential letters of protest at least one of which had come from the Balrothery Poor Law Guardians. On 17 February, the guardians received a letter from the office of the Secretary of the Admiralty, acknowledging receipt of their letter, but that was the end of their correspondence and involvement in the affair.

In the end, the objections and connections of the likes of Lord Talbot de Malahide probably held far greater weight than the potential profitability to any private company of the reclaimed land, and the scheme got bogged down in the House of Lords. Further attempts would be made in 1866 and 1883 to revive the project, but neither would prove successful. Kelly's vigilance had paid off. Eight hundred families had been spared the ordeal of the workhouse.

By the early 1930s, the area around the Rogerstown Estuary had changed considerably. A general movement towards consolidation in farm size had seen the myriad of small tenant farmers largely disappear from the estuary. Those that remained had lost their taste for shellfish and no longer relied exclusively on collected seaweed for fertiliser.

With unemployment and emigration levels rising daily, the saltmarshes of the Malahide and Rogerstown estuaries once again began to be viewed as 'waste' land that if reclaimed could provide valuable employment in the area. Biodiversity, as both a word and a concept, had yet to penetrate the public imagination.

In January 1935, therefore, it came as little surprise to anyone in Fingal when a motion to reclaim the estuary was proposed, debated, and passed on the floor of Seanad Eireann. The motion was tabled by Killarney-born John Joseph Conahan, a member of the senate then resident at New lawn House and Farm, in Ballyboughal, north County Dublin.

Counihan, at that time a member of Fine Gael, but due shortly to leave the party to serve as an independent, had come to Ballyboughal in 1915 by way of Kildare, where he had formerly been a tillage farmer. Since arriving in Ballyboughal, however, he had concentrated his efforts on raising pedigree and commercial livestock.

Counihan was well placed to understand the potential value of the land. His motion, however, had not been tabled from commercial motives but in response to a public invitation from the Board of

Works for suggestions regarding potential relief schemes.

Subsequent to the motion, at an undetermined date, an experimental one-metre high embankment was constructed along a three-quarter-mile stretch of the south bank of the estuary to the west of the railway bridge, and an attempt was made to reclaim a limited amount of the tidal wetlands for agricultural use. The reclaimed land appears to have been used primarily for pasture and forestry, but to have remained prone to flooding.

A much larger, and more successful, amount of reclamation took place on the north shore and facilitated the creation of the Balleally Landfill (now Rogerstown Park). This section has today been permanently reclaimed. The south shore section of the embankment, close to Turvey Park was, on the other hand, levelled by Fingal County Council as part of a biodiversity program in 2015, to allow exceptionally high tides to flood the area as they had presumably done in the past.

Turvey Woods at Rogerstown – Returning to its natural state.

Despite several attempts to do so, the slobs of the Rogerstown Estuary were never fully reclaimed and remain today a valued local amenity and an internationally important wildlife reserve and wetland bird sanctuary, providing safe roosting sites for thousands of wintering wildfowl and waders.

THE DISPENSARY COMMITTEE

DESPITE HIS INTERVENTION in the Rogerstown embankment controversy, William Kelly's political career only really began in earnest in 1866, with the passing of a new Public Health Act.

Introduced following an outbreak of cholera in England, the act not only expanded the role of Poor Law dispensary districts to include matters of sanitation and disease prevention, but also allowed the devolution of some Poor Law Union powers and responsibilities to elected local representatives in the form of Dispensary District Committees of Management.

Every medical officer of a dispensary district now became the district's de-facto sanitary officer and, together with the Committee of Management, responsible for the discovery, inspection and removal of nuisances, the supply of pure water, the making or repairing of sewers and drains, and the administration of the sanitary laws within the district. In Fingal, six dispensary districts were created with headquarters in Balbriggan, Malahide, Oldtown, Rush, Skerries, and Swords. The Portrane peninsula formed part of the Swords Dispensary District.

With each dispensary district now being run by its own local Committee of Management, a place on the dispensary committee gave the elected official not just a high profile in his locality, but a chance to truly make a difference in the lives of his friends and neighbours. Whether it had been its intention or not, the 1866 act turned the men of the dispensary committees into the first truly *local* politicians, the precursors of today's county councillors.

1866 was also, coincidentally, the same year that five young men lost their lives to hydrogen sulphide poisoning in Donabate. They had been cleaning out a liquid manure tank in the bullock yard adjoining Newbridge House. Four of them had died attempting to rescue Patrick Smith, the first of the young men to get into trouble.

Patrick was just nineteen. When he lost consciousness, twenty-one-year-old Michael Shannon, went in to get him out, only to be overcome by the gases himself. The other boys who died, all aged between twenty and twenty-five, were Luke Flynn, Maurice Collins, and James Wren. All had gone into the tank attempting to rescue their friends.

Michael Shannon's father, Larry, arrived late on the scene and, utterly distraught, went into the tank to attempt the rescue of his son. He was only saved from certain death by virtue of an act of bravery by a visiting carpenter, Thomas Redmond, who went in after him and dragged his unconscious body out. Apart from Patrick Smith, all of the boys had grown up together in the village of Donabate, in cottages that were but a stone's throw apart.

The tragedy devasted the parish; all the more so for the public nature of the aftermath. In the roadside burial ground that surrounded the Catholic chapel five graves could not be dug discreetly, nor could the solemn procession of inquest jurors moving from cottage to cottage to view the bodies be shielded from voyeuristic eyes.

Donabate was a tiny, tight-knit community. Everyone knew everyone. The Kellys would have known the dead boys, and they would have known their parents, especially Tom Wren, the man most badly affected by the loss. Tom's son, James, had only been in the job two days and was the chief support to his parents and two younger sisters. Just seven days previous, Tom had buried a twelve-year-old daughter. Two children lost, seven days apart.

On Monday, 11 September, the boys were laid to rest and the entire village choked in a cloud of uncomprehending sorrow. Nobody, but nobody, was left untouched; not those who lived in Donabate or Portrane and had personal connections to the families concerned, nor the vast crowds from further afield who had travelled to the funeral to be a part of the spectacle, nor even the many, many others who would read dramatic, at times melodramatic, accounts of the tragedy in the newspapers over the course of the week that followed. The widespread publicity did at least lead to a collection being raised for the families of the deceased.

The pall of communal grief had yet to lift from the village when, just eight days later, the Kellys were next to be plunged helplessly into the mire. Mary Jane Kelly's live-in niece, Mary Jane Shanks, died from what was described on her death certificate as a 'pulmonary disease' that had been 'three years certified'. She was just thirty-one years of age, still unmarried, and still living at Middlefield. It was the third funeral in the village in the space of three weeks, and all seven of the deceased had died tragically young.

It was never expressly stated. But, given the circumstances and the young age at which she died, it is possible that the root cause of Mary Jane Shanks' illness had been her youthful living conditions in Dublin. Respiratory diseases were quite common amongst the poor of Dublin, and living conditions in the city's tenement buildings were amongst the worst in Western Europe. Squalor, malnourishment, and disease were rife, and obstructive airway disease quite common amongst the children of malnourished mothers.

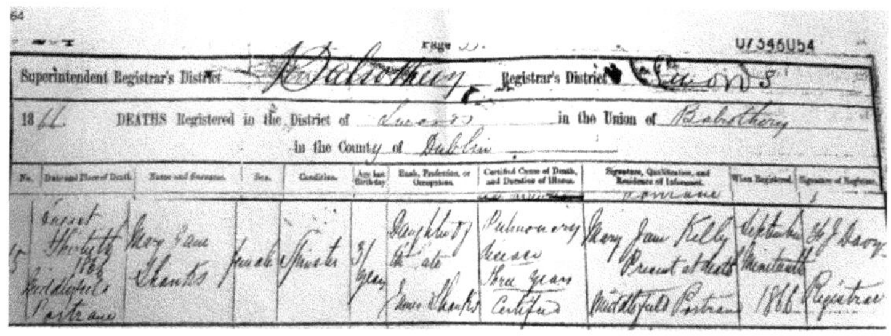
Superintendent Registrar's District Balrothery Registrar's District

18 66. DEATHS Registered in the District of in the Union of Balrothery in the County of Dublin

No.	Date and Place of Death	Name and Surname	Sex	Condition	Age last Birthday	Rank, Profession, or Occupation	Certified Cause of Death, and Duration of Illness	Signature, Qualification, and Residence of Informant	When Registered	Signature of Registrar
5	August Thirtieth 1866 Middlefield Portrane	Mary Jane Shanks	Female	Spinster	31 years	Daughter of the late James Shanks	Pulmonary disease three years Certified	Mary Jane Kelly Present at death Middlefield Portrane	September Nineteenth 1866	Registrar

Mary Jane Shanks' Death Certificate

The clean air of Portrane had obviously done little for Mary Jane Shank's health and, despite the care of her aunt and adopted 'sister', she had managed to survive just six winters at Middlefield. Following a funeral mass at Middlefield House, she was taken to Glasnevin and buried alongside her father, James, in the grave that William Kelly had purchased for him in 1860.

For Mary Jane Derrick, the loss must have been especially cruel. Having already lost both her parents and her foster parents, she had now lost the closest thing she had ever had to a sister. She was twenty-eight now, and also unmarried. She had only William and Mary Jane Kelly to turn to in her grief.

One cannot help but wonder, given the timing, if there had been something about Mary Jane Shanks' suffering that William Kelly believed to have been preventable – something, perhaps, that had left him with some residual feeling of responsibility – because, shortly before her death, having never in his life before sought public office, he suddenly put himself forward for election to the management committee of the Swords Dispensary District. In so doing he effectively replaced John McAllister, a neighbour whose lands abutted his own at Middlefield. This committee, responsible for the medical care of the inhabitants of the Portrane Peninsula and the greater Swords region in general, endowed its members with a considerable public profile, weighty responsibilities, and medical privileges.

Subsequently elected, along with four others, Kelly would devote much of the next thirteen years of his life to that role, finding himself re-elected on an annual basis to a committee responsible for the organisation and management of the medical and sanitary services of the district. On the last Saturday of every month, he would diligently drive his carriage to the dispensary in Swords for the monthly meetings of the Dispensary Committee, at least until 1879, when his health, and the health of his wife, began to fail.

This was no easy role to fulfil and Kelly would have been subject to all manner of demanding representation and lobbying by his 'constituents'. On top of all that he would have been required to help oversee the development of health and sanitation services in the area, including the management of smallpox vaccination programs, the treatment of mental illnesses, and various dealings with other public bodies such as the Office of Public Works.

There were, however, 'perks' to the job, the most regularly abused of which was the distribution of dispensary tickets by committee men. A 'black' relief ticket allowed a patient to visit a doctor at the dispensary and receive medical advice and medicine free of charge; a 'red' visiting ticket, intended for those too ill to travel to the dispensary, required the dispensary doctor to visit the patient at home (the ticket names reflecting the colour of the ink used in their printing).

The decision as to who was entitled to a ticket was left to the discretion of the management committee without any guidelines as to decision making. What constituted a 'poor person' was never adequately defined, and committee men who ran their own businesses were often reluctant to refuse tickets to good customers. As a result, the distribution of tickets, and most especially of red tickets, often became a matter of personal largesse rather than actual need.

The widespread abuse of 'red' tickets was particularly problematic for the dispensary doctors. It obliged them, as one correspondent complained in a letter to *The Lancet*, to:

'... go at once to the patient's house, however far that patient may live or whatever the hour of the day. No matter what private business he may have, the dispensary medical officer must put all aside to attend to the red ticket. All his other and paying patients must be neglected so as to obey the red ticket summons.'

All too frequently tickets were issued to people who were perfectly capable of paying for the service and, as the very people who were abusing the ticketing service were the same people who controlled their employment, doctors were loath to complain. Kept in a state of perpetual thraldom to the committee men who decided who the doctor should see and when they would be seen, they had effectively been reduced to a tool of medical patronage.

Such was the power of the committee men that,

even without resorting to summary dismissal, they could destroy a difficult medical officer's life. One commonly reported method was to issue a continuous series of red tickets to boys who would watch the medical officer and ensure that no sooner had he returned home from one red ticket visit than he was presented with another, forcing him to go out again on visits that often turned out to be false alarms.

Some of the more widely publicised abuses of the time included landlords who gave out tickets to their servants, and retail tradesmen and publicans who left entire books of signed tickets with their staff to distribute amongst their customers. The medical officers may have despaired at such abuses, but amongst the general public attitudes were much more relaxed and the abuse of dispensary committee status was generally seen as akin to a time-honoured prerogative. The upshot of it all was that if your own village or parish was not represented on this committee, it laboured at a distinct disadvantage with regard to access to medical services compared to one that was.

As a member of the Swords Dispensary Committee, William Kelly would have had a very high profile in the villages of Donabate and Portrane during these years and yielded a great deal of power and influence. Almost every 'poor person' in the district would have had cause at one stage or another to call to his house to appeal for a dispensary ticket and he would have had a great deal of influence over the type of medical and dental care that they, his servants and his family received.

His newly acquired status, alas, came too late for Mary Jane Shanks.

Another, albeit minor, contributory factor in Kelly's decision to involve himself in matters of public health may well have been the risk to the farming industry caused by rinderpest, a morbillivirus nicknamed the

'Russian Plague'. The disease, closely related to measles, had killed over a quarter of a million animals, primarily cattle, in Britain the previous year and had been prevented from entering Ireland largely through the efforts of his old friend, Edward Purdon, joint owner of *The Farmer's Gazette*.

In 1865 Purdon had cautioned guests at a banquet in Clonmel that if the epidemic was unleashed in Ireland up to thirteen million cattle would be lost, resulting in 'national bankruptcy'. Later, as Hon. Secretary of the Cattle Plague Committee, Purdon had helped to co-ordinate efforts to prevent the disease from gaining a foothold in Ireland, efforts for which William Kelly was especially grateful. He had lived through one famine. He did not want to live through another.

Purdon had been a good friend and loyal ally to Kelly over the years and when he found himself in financial difficulty Kelly was not slow in coming forward. In both 1859 and 1866, when committees were formed to raise funds for Purdon in recognition of all that he had done over the years in the cause of Irish agriculture, Kelly made the maximum donation. In November 1866, he even wrote a letter to the organising committee that was subsequently published on the front page of the *Evening Freeman*:

SIR–

Had the rinderpest established itself in Ireland as it did in England, the result would have been disastrous. The tillage farmers would have first been demolished, and the graziers and landlords would soon follow. Under God's providence, I believe that Ireland owes her immunity from the rinderpest in a great degree to Mr Purdon's exertions, and I, as a tillage farmer, therefore, gladly add my mite to the Purdon testimonial, a cheque for which (1l.) I enclose.

I may be wrong; but I think it was unwise of the committee to limit the subscription to 1l. The landlords and graziers should be allowed to come forward with their 5l. or 10. Or 30l., and render the testimonial in some measure commensurate with the benefits they derived from Mr Purdon's exertions.

I am, Sir,
Your very obedient servant,
WILLIAM KELLY

Whatever it was that provoked William Kelly into seeking a seat on the Dispensary Committee, for the next thirteen years he would strive to ensure that the Portrane peninsula was never left unrepresented. Unlike so many other committee men across the country, Kelly had nothing to gain by his service. Nothing, that is, but the one thing he had so desperately craved his entire life – respect.

LAND AND LAW

THE YEARS RAN on and the world changed, both in the factories and in the fields. And it wasn't just the machinery that was constantly changing, the faces changed, too, it being an accepted part of farming life that labourers and servants would die, retire, or marry and move away.

The new faces to arrive at Middlefield were Owen and Elizabeth McGorish, siblings from County Monaghan. It is unlikely that they were residing at Middlefield house. More likely they took the servants' quarters in the annexe to the rear of the house or the living quarters above the coach house.

Given their origins, it is entirely possible that the McGorishs were distantly related to William and in the years to come Middlefield House would pass to Elizabeth, following her marriage to Charlie McAllister, third son of their near neighbour, John McAllister. For the time being, however, they were fresh and energetic young faces. New blood. After the death of Mary Jane Shanks, their arrival represented something of a tonic.

Across the road at Mount Evans, things were

changing too. When he had first been spotted using a mowing machine, Kelly had been tending to the lawns at Portrane House, suggesting that even then he was still on good terms with his landlord. All that changed, however, in 1864, when Joshua Evans died and George Evans' health began to fail, compelling him to move to France and entrust the running of the estate to the Hon. St. John Butler of Walshestown, third son of Baron Dunboyne. Butler had heretofore been managing the estates of Sir Roger Palmer at Lusk.

Following Butler's appointment as steward, Kelly's relationship with his landlord became strained. The cause of their falling out was the thorny matter of game, specifically the rabbits and hares that were crossing the demesne boundaries and devouring Kelly's crops. The Evans estate was currently being utilised primarily as a holiday home for shooting parties and, to maximise game, Butler had allowed the numbers to run riot.

The story of animals trespassing on crops was as old as Cain and Abel: Cain the settled farmer and Abel the keeper of sheep. Substitute rabbits for sheep, and little in the moral of the story changes. The fate of Cain, forever denied the fruits of the soil and sent into wandering exile, served as a warning to the tillers of the soil against taking matters into their own hands.

Unlike birds, for which there was a definitive season, there was no closed season on rabbits and no incentive to cull. Kelly sought mediation with Evans and received a written assurance, in April of 1866, that Evans would compensate him for any loss to his crops. Since then, the annual damage had far exceeded anything that Evans was willing to pay, and Kelly had had enough.

The end of the Crimean War and the free importation of corn had run down the price of cereal crops and Kelly was struggling. He could not afford to be losing crops to rabbits. The law surrounding the matter of game, however, had never been properly tested in Ireland and Kelly had been reluctant to start shooting rabbits on land he was leasing from Evans for fear of landing himself in trouble with the law. His only recourse was to sue for greater damages.

This was an historic moment in Irish legal history. No Irish tenant had ever dared to sue a landlord over the matter of game before and the case was widely reported in the press. Not half as widely, however, as the paramilitary activities of the Irish Republican Brotherhood.

On 5 March 1867, members of this movement staged a rebellion. The main battle took place at Tallaght, at that time a small village 20km outside the city of Dublin. Thousands of young Dubliners on their way to a muster of the Irish Republican Brotherhood were intercepted by armed police who had been pre-warned of their assembly. Skirmishes also took place in Cork, Limerick, Tipperary, Monaghan, and Louth, but the rebellion quickly fell apart and was over before it had properly begun.

Following the failure of the uprising, Isaac Butt, a Donegal-born barrister and former Member of Parliament for Youghal, decided to defend the rebels in court. Prior to 1845, Butt had been both a committed Unionist and a member of the Orange Order. His experiences during the famine, however, had altered his outlook and he was now the leading campaigner for a federal political system that would allow Ireland a greater degree of self-rule.

Butt's two published books, *Plea for the Celtic Race* and *Irish People and Irish Land*, furthermore, had excited enough attention and support to allow him to establish a new Tenants' League, which petered out following the introduction of the Land Act in 1868. Always willing to tackle landmark cases, that same year Isaac Butt became William Kelly's barrister.

One of the earliest members of Butt's Tenants' League, had been William Kelly's friend, Andrew Kettle. Born into a Jacobean-style manor at Swords in north

County Dublin, Kettle had been educated at Ireland's most prestigious Catholic boarding school, Clongowes Wood College. He lived just across the estuary in Malahide and his mother was a Donabate woman called Alice Kavanaugh.

Following the collapse of Butt's Tenants' League, Kettle got in touch with William Kelly and Kelly's friend and neighbour, Thomas McCourt of Lanestown. Kettle knew both men from their activities in the Balrothery Poor Law Union and felt confident of receiving a sympathetic hearing. Together they managed to recruit several other large farmers from the surrounding area and to form a County Dublin Tenant's Defence Association. From the outset, they had Butt's support. He even attended some of the new association's meetings.

Kelly liked Butt. He was a fellow northerner, a plain-spoken man with an accent not a million miles from his own. Here, at long last, was a politician he could understand and trust; a Protestant, like the Rev. Hickey, who for five years had been like a surrogate father to him. Good men, despite the heresy. At Butt's suggestion Kettle and Kelly decided to form a national body, the Central Tenants Defence Association, in which they both immediately took leading roles.

In the *Dublin Evening Post* of 31 July 1868, in an article dealing with the history of Wexford Agriculture and in particular the Bannow Farm School, a correspondent signing himself simply as 'An Outsider' described former pupil, William Kelly, as 'one of the distinguished professional agriculturists in Great Britain or Ireland and one of the most successful practical farmers of the present time.' Kelly, he went on to say, was the originator of a 'designed system of grass crop culture to which the world is now so much indebted'.

Still very much renowned as an agriculturist, William Kelly, was slowly becoming equally, if not better known as an agrarian activist. His legal case, when it eventually came to court, would not just be historic, it would be high profile and a significant milestone in the fight for tenants' rights. Hardly surprising then, that when he found himself in need of a barrister, it should be Isaac Butt who represented him.

On 6 December 1869, the disposable chattels of Portrane House and Demesne were finally sold by George Evans who was 'about to reside on the continent'. Such was the scope of the auction that the Dublin and Drogheda Railway Company consented to stop the 9:45 a.m. train at Donabate for potential bidders. Everything from harvested crops to livestock, from fine wines to horses and ponies, from dairy equipment to household furniture was sold, along with all of the hardware and equipment that William Kelly had once used to run the farm as a thriving agricultural enterprise. It was a quick sale. Everything went for cash.

George Evans' departure for the continent, however, did little to accelerate the legal process and it took several years for Kelly's claim against him to come to court. When it finally did, it caused the expected stir. *The Farmer's Gazette* expressed it thus:

'Those who are in the habit of reading agricultural journals published in England and Scotland are aware that the subject which excites the greatest amount of interest at the present time is the game question, or the over-preservation of game, leading to serious injury to growing crops. It is, indeed, a hard case when a man has to pay a high rent, and incur heavy expenses in cultivation, for the purpose apparently of enjoying the privilege of feeding hares and rabbits which he dare not touch, and which another man claims as his peculiar property.

That great injury is annually sustained by farmers in those parts of the kingdom where game is preserved with great strictness is a well-known fact, and the injury caused by the over-preservation of game has been vastly increased since the barbarous, butcherly, and unsportsmanlike practice of battu-shooting has become prevalent. To get up a large head of game is the great object of every keeper, no matter what injury may be thereby inflicted on the neighbouring farmers; and so far is it carried that in not a few instances the truly manly sport of fox-hunting has been abandoned owing to the foxes having been trapped, shot and poisoned by game-keepers who care more for hares and rabbits – the latter as their own perquisite – than for foxes . . . While actions at law, arising from the damage done by game, are common in Great Britain, they have, until now, been unknown, so far as we are aware, in Ireland.

Last week, however, an important case of this kind was brought before the Chief Baron and a special jury in the Court of Exchequer, Dublin. As the case of Kelly v. Evans has been the first of the kind in Ireland, so we hope it will be the last we shall have occasion to record in our columns; and we trust that fair sport, to which no one objects, will continue to be, as it has ever been, the rule in Ireland.'

That article would be one of the last to be published by *The Farmer's Gazette*, which ceased publishing that very same year. Edward Purdon was now Lord Mayor of Dublin and intent on a career in politics. His time as a magazine editor was over and he and Kelly slowly drifted apart.

As for the court case, Kelly, with no little assistance from Isaac Butt, eventually prevailed, and while he didn't get everything that he wanted, he wasn't quite finished with Evans just yet. With the estate's lands next in line to be sold Kelly decided to surrender his lease and take advantage of a more recently enacted piece of legislation, the waters having already been tested for him by another good friend, Maurice Butterly.

On 1 July 1871, Butterly, a tenant of Sir Charles Domvile, applied to register improvements to his farm at Santry, in north Dublin, under Section 6 of the Landlord and Tenant Act of 1870. This act allowed tenants to file a schedule in the Landed Estates Court specifying the improvements made in order to have them accepted as prima facie evidence in future claims for compensation at such time as they may be evicted or chose to quit their holdings. William Kelly, described in the court reports as 'an extensive farmer', was called as a witness in support of Butterly's claim and, in November of the following year, Kelly followed Butterly's example and filed a suit of his own.

The root of these court cases reached back to 1868 when the Liberal Party, under the leadership of William Gladstone, was elected on a platform of land reform. Gladstone's attention had been sharpened by the failed Fenian rebellion of the previous year and by the opinions of the president of the Board of Trade, John Bright, who believed that the solution to the Irish land question lay in transforming the tenants into owners.

While sympathetic to the plight of Irish tenants, Gladstone was forever wary of diluting the laws concerning private property and, unwilling to commit political suicide to resolve the problem, strived to find a compromise. His Landlord and Tenant (Ireland) Act of 1870, managed to reform some contractual aspects of land leases, but it failed to go quite as far as Bright, or indeed the Irish MPs, had wanted.

Prior to the new act, any improvement made by a tenant to any Irish landlord's property outside of the province of Ulster would be accredited to the landlord, giving little incentive to the tenant to maintain the property. Under the new act, tenants gained increased security and compensation for improvements made to a farm, but only at such time as they were evicted or surrendered their lease.

Amongst the improvements for which Kelly was

claiming were 'the building of a dwelling house and large number of offices, the sinking of pumps, erection of stone walls, planting and building of ditches and fences, the making of drains, blasting and removing rocks, stubbing and clearing away old bushes, and making in fact a quantity of new land.' Evans contested the dating of a number of these works and denied that others represented any real improvement at all.

Despite Kelly's protests, many of Evans' points were upheld by the chairman, but Kelly was not about to let an unjust decision slip by unchallenged. Despite the costs that would inevitably accrue, he appealed the judgement. There was more at stake here than money. He was angry, and he was bitter. He was no longer willing to be dismissed or ignored by the landed establishment.

Kelly's legal battle under the terms of Section 6 of the Landlord and Tenant Act, was not unique, but it was followed very closely in Portrane, where Kelly's status in the local community had recently been underscored by his appointment as monitor to the two local primary schools that had been founded by his old employer, Sophia Evans, and, indeed, in the County Dublin Tenants Defence Association, where he was slowly becoming a regular presence in the chair.

Before the appeal could be heard, however, Kelly took to the newspapers, the target of his vitriol being the lame excuses the landlords of Ireland were proffering in justification of their decision to raise rents, suggesting, perhaps, that he himself had been a victim. The letter was published on New Year's Day, 1873, on page six of the *Freeman's Journal.* In case anyone had forgotten him, he introduced himself as 'Mr William Kelly, Portrane, Donabate, author of "Villa Farmer," &c.'

'A correct knowledge of the gross rental of the lands of any country has been held by the best agricultural

writers to be of very great importance to its inhabitants. It occurs to me that such knowledge is of greater importance to both the owners and occupiers of land in Ireland at the present time than it ever was before.

As an humble tillage farmer, I feel the greatest diffidence in offering my opinion on this great subject. At present the tillage farmer's intellect is clouded, if by nothing else, by the constant rains, which it has please Providence to pour upon him, almost unceasingly, for nearly the last thirteen months, retarding his operations in the field and blighting and destroying his crops.

Besides, the tillage farmer's education is very limited, and it is only his practical experience that could warrant him at all in offering his opinion on such an important subject; and it is, therefore, in the hope that men of more experience and more intelligence than I possess will take part in the elucidation of this question that I offer the following observations.

That it is contemplated by landlords to make a great increase to the rent of their lands as the opportunity offers is evident from what we see and hear of every day. In this immediate district a few cases have occurred where the rents have been increased 27 shillings per Irish acre, the previous rent having been considered a rack rent. Such an increase at such a time is by far a more convenient method of "contracting" tenants out of the property conferred on them by the Land Act than any mere bargain or agreement.

It is asserted by landlords and their agents that rents should increase because the price of the produce of the land had increased; because, in fact, the "times are better," and also because the rents of land in Ireland are much lower than the rents of land in England or Scotland. These propositions require proof. That "times are better" as regards the tillage farmer, I deny; on the contrary, his position is getting worse.

I have been engaged in farming during the last 40 years in the county Dublin, and, with the exception of a few years, the price of grain and other products of tillage have been as high as at present. The price of young stock and of butter is higher; but the sales of these by the tillage farmer is so small as scarcely to affect his circumstances.

On the other hand, it is the inferior lands, not only in county Dublin, but all over Ireland, that are in tillage. Labour, considering quantity and quality, is more than double the cost it was 20 years ago, or any time previously. Blacksmiths, carpenters, harness makers, and every tradesman the farmer employs must be paid a great deal more than usual, because "labour is so high."

Everything the farmer requires for himself or his family must be bought at a greatly increased price, because, "labour is so high," and I suppose that rents must also be increased because "labour is so high;" but the farmer cannot go to the corn market and say, I must get the price I demand for my wheat, oats and barley, because "labour is so high".

No, California, Russia and Germany, &c, have settled the price he must take. The "strike" system is available to every class in society but the farmer, who is injured by all strikes, but must be content to take things as Providence sends them.

This present year there is a good price for potatoes, but the majority of farmers have very few to sell, and since 1845 he has lost on an average half that crop by blight every year. This year (I speak of the county Dublin) much of the cereal crops were unusually badly saved, and are as low in price as almost any time within my memory. The produce is also small. Buck wheat, grown largely in this district, which used to produce thirteen to twenty barrels per Irish acre, gives this year from four to ten barrels of very inferior quality. These circumstances do not call for or justify an increased rent, so far as the tillage farmer is concerned at present, because with him the times are certainly not better.'

Kelly went on to question the landlords' audacity in drawing comparisons between rent prices in rich countries like England with those of an impoverished country like Ireland, where the quality of the land was generally much poorer. He produced facts, figures, and statistics to support his arguments, even quoting from the book of Genesis (Gen. chap xlvii, v, xxiv.) a habit he doubtlessly picked up at Bannow, the quoting of Old Testament not being a particularly characteristic trait of Roman Catholics of the day, whose religion was more firmly rooted in the New Testament than the Old. Then again, William Kelly had always, in many ways, been a very Protestant Catholic. Twenty-four days after the publication of Kelly's letter, the County Dublin Tenants Defence Association admitted no less than fifty new members.

Kelly's appeal was finally heard in May 1873. The judge, Baron Deasy, adjourned the case for a day to visit the works in question and see for himself what all the fuss was about. Upon his return to chambers, he upheld most, but not all, of Kelly's appeals. Despite the qualified victory, Kelly once again left the courtroom with the smarting sense of having been cheated.

Things began to change in the Kelly household shortly after that when Mary Jane Derrick began to attract the attention of local widower and neighbour, John McAllister, a man eighteen years her senior. McAllister knew Kelly from his work with the Balrothery Poor Law Union, where he had sat on various committees, Kelly having effectively replaced him on the dispensary committee in 1866.

John McAllister's wife, Bridget (née Keeling), had died in 1870 at the age of forty, just three months after giving birth to their only daughter, Jane. She had given her husband eight sons prior to that. Her two eldest sons, John junior and Willie, had emigrated to Argentina two years before her death to join John's brother Joseph on his *estancia* in Pergamino. The next two, Charlie and Christopher, were old enough to look after themselves. But that still left John with four children of twelve and younger to raise alone.

John McAllister needed a wife, and his children needed mothering. He began, therefore, to set his cap at Mary Jane Derrick. What's more, despite the inevitable baggage he would bring to the relationship, she appeared to be warming to him.

HOME RULE

IN 1870, KELLY'S barrister, Isaac Butt (above), founded the Home Government Association with the stated purpose of repealing the Act of Union and reinstating an Irish parliament that would be based in Ireland, passing laws separately from the main Parliament in London.

Butt had already won the admiration of Catholics with his impassioned defence of Young Ireland and Fenian prisoners, and William Kelly had gotten to know and admire him through his own court case and Butt's attendance at meetings of both the County Dublin Tenants Defence Association and the Central Tenants Defence Association, in which Kelly was now playing a prominent role.

Butt's Home Government Association proved popular with both Catholics and Protestants, but thus far the Catholic Bishops had kept themselves at arm's length. Further hampering its broader appeal was the fact that the association had a rather exclusive membership. Butt, belatedly recognising the fact, set out to remedy it. In November 1873, he organised a four-day conference at the Rotunda that was attended by twenty-five members of parliament and nine hundred delegates. They voted to turn the Home Government Association into the Home Rule League, open to all and sundry. Having formed a new party, the next step was to select electoral candidates and get them elected.

However, on 24 January, Gladstone suddenly decided to dissolve parliament, leaving his rivals in a race against time to organise for a February election. With the Home Rule League having only been in existence for three weeks, it found itself with insufficient funds to fight an election. Nevertheless, with the tenant farmers deciding to have their say in the selection of Home Rule candidates, the issues of home rule and land reform had become one and, seizing the opportunity, the party decided to contest the election.

An urgent invitation was now issued by the Home Rule League to the Catholic clergy, pleading with them to take their proper place alongside the people. Home rule, they contended, was the *only* hope for 'religion, order, and peace'. On the back of that invitation, William Kelly and several of his colleagues in the County Dublin Tenants Defence Association immediately attempted to procure the active endorsement of the head of the Catholic Church in

Ireland, Cardinal Paul Cullen.

Cullen was one of the intellectual élites of the Catholic Church and a man with a rather chequered history of engagement with the tenants' rights movement. The seventy-year-old Kildare man was the first Irishman ever to achieve the rank of cardinal and the man who had crafted the formula for papal infallibility at the First Vatican Council. Responsible for initiating the practice of Irish priests wearing Roman collars and being called 'Father' instead of 'Mister', he was a man as demanding of ceremonial respect as Richard III had once been of magisterial reverence.

Cardinal Paul Cullen

Perhaps the most important figure in Irish politics since the death of Daniel O'Connell, Cullen's hierarchy of loyalty put church first and country second. Suspicious of secret societies, he had waged a public campaign against both the Young Ireland and Fenian movements that the current leader of the Home Rule League, Isaac Butt, had so famously and eloquently defended in court. Back in 1855, furthermore, it had been Frederick Lucas' attempts to bring criticism of Cullen to Rome that had scuppered the first Tenant Right League. Cullen was a formidable political operator. If Kelly and his colleagues were going to approach him, they needed to tread lightly and bow respectfully when they kissed his episcopal ring.

On hearing of their request, Cullen granted the delegation an audience and, led by Kelly, a delegation comprised of Andrew Kettle, James O'Neill, and Charles Reilly, went to see if they could persuade the cardinal to offer some public sympathy to their cause. The suddenness of the election, Kelly explained, had hampered their hopes of reaching the electors of the country in time. If they were to impart their message with any great force, they would need the assistance of the Catholic clergy. Rightly or wrongly, he continued, his Eminence was held to be opposed to priests taking any active part in politics. Surely the current circumstances warranted an exception?

Cullen denied that he had ever issued any orders against clergy sympathising with the people under suitable circumstances, but he *was* opposed to them leading from the front. If the delegation could find a man or two who were up to the standard of the present company on the questions of land and home rule, and who were up to his own standards with regard to education, he would do what he could to facilitate them. If they could let him have the names by Thursday, he promised, he would arrange it so that they could hold their campaign meetings the following Sunday in every Catholic churchyard in the county.

'I hope,' he then said, looking directly at William Kelly, 'that you do not expect me to appear openly in this contest?'

Before the plain-speaking Kelly could offer his usual

frank opinion, Andrew Kettle cut in. 'I think, your Eminence,' he said, 'it would be bad enough to be beaten without you, but it would be most unwise and impolitic to have you publicly beaten'.

Getting suitable candidates at such short notice presented a difficulty. Someone suggested young Charles Stewart Parnell, of Avondale in County Wicklow, who had already spoken publicly on the home rule issue. Kelly must have had mixed feelings about this. Charles' father was the same John Parnell who had objected to Sophia Evans' posthumous gratuity to Kelly in 1853. Nevertheless, a deputation was duly dispatched and Parnell, a half-American, Cambridge-educated agnostic, gave his consent. Despite shaking the landlord monopoly, however, Parnell failed to get elected, losing out by 1,141 votes to 2,122. As a gesture of goodwill, and of his commitment to the cause, Parnell paid his own election expenses.

That sudden election, of February 1874, saw Butt's Home Rule League win almost half the seats in parliament and, inspired by their success, William Kelly finally decided to become a paid-up member. He was admitted that April and barely a year later Irish newspapers would be recording his attendance at meetings of the Parliamentary Land Committee.

Parnell, in the meantime, had won a by-election caused by the death of John Martin and was returned to Parliament as the MP for County Meath. He spent most of the parliamentary season in London but, whenever he returned to Ireland, he made a point of attending as many of the tenants' rights meetings as he could, renewing, perhaps, in the process, a passing acquaintance with William Kelly that went back to his childhood. Kelly's former employer, Sophia Evans, was a grand-aunt of Parnell and had been godmother to his short-lived brother, William. The Parnells had also been frequent visitors to Portrane during Sophia's lifetime and William's tenure as steward.

At the age of sixty-eight, William Kelly was still brimming with passion for the cause of tenant farmers. By May of the following year, he would also be serving with Isaac Butt and Andrew Kettle on the council of the Home Rule League. His transformation from land agent to an agrarian activist was now complete.

AT LAST - A WEDDING

SHE HAD LIVED with them for fifteen years, and during that time had shared almost every moment of their waking lives. They had become surrogate parents to her, and she almost a daughter to them. So, when the time came to walk her down the aisle of the old Catholic church in Donabate, there would have been no man more proud, or more relieved, to see his young charge settled than William Kelly, nor any bride more grateful, or fortunate, to have found a respectable husband than Mary Jane Derrick.

She was thirty-two, late by the standards of the day for marriage. The decision to accept John McAllister's proposal, nevertheless, could not have been easy. He had already made a life, and a family, with someone else, and his in-laws lived locally. Too close, in fact, not to interfere in the upbringing of their grandchildren, should the mood take them.

To further complicate matters, John McAllister's late wife was but five years in her grave; scarcely long enough for *him* to have fully dealt with the grief or for *her* to lose the suspicion that old memories were still too fresh not to be compared to the new. But he was a good man, and she was realistic. She would have known the enormity of the responsibilities involved in accepting him, and, for that matter, his children.

John McAllister's eldest two sons, John and Willie, had already emigrated to Argentina. The eldest remaining son, Charlie, was now twenty-two and mooching around twenty-one-year-old Elizabeth McGorish. As for Christopher, he was fast approaching his eighteenth birthday and his sights were set on Australia. The remaining children were very young and would require skilful nurturing. There was George (12), James (9), Patrick (7), and John's only daughter, Jane (4).

But the Kellys were getting old and Mary Jane Derrick could never have aspired to run a farm by herself. At thirty-two she might never have gotten another offer, or at least one as good as this. And so, on the morning of Tuesday, 12 January 1875, the Kelly and McAllister households donned their Sunday best and drove in their freshly polished carriages to the Roman Catholic chapel in Donabate, where John McAllister and Mary Jane Derrick were joined in holy matrimony by the Parish Priest, Fr. Michael O'Sullivan. After the wedding, the newlyweds came to live at Middlefield and if the house had ever rung with the sound of children's voices during William and Mary Jane Kelly's lifetime, it would have been in the years immediately following this wedding.

A mere five years after the death of their mother, when the memory of her was still fresh in their hearts and minds, the McAllister children found themselves presented with a replacement to whom they would now be expected to look for physical and emotional support. It would be unusual, to say the least, if they had not been gradually introduced to their father's intended in the months or years preceding the marriage, and equally unusual if they had been unanimous in their support of their father's new bride or consistently respectful of her authority. For the new and inexperienced Mrs McAllister, the parenting of young children would present a formidable challenge, but she at least had some understanding of what they were going through. Young James was the same age now as she had been when she herself had been orphaned and forced to go live with another family. And she had not just faced this upheaval once in her life, she had endured it twice.

That said, Mary Jane Derrick had no first-hand experience of raising children, let alone three boisterous young boys, and she had lacked a mother-figure in her life since the age of four. After fifteen years living with the Kellys, the only thing she was truly qualified for was the role of a farmer's wife. Motherhood, she would have to learn on the hoof.

On top of all that, the new Mrs McAllister would have to deal with the ghost of the old, whose family were still grandparents, aunts, and uncles, to her new husband's children. She would be regularly reminded of the dead woman's virtues, would have to fight the sense of being her substitute, and would have to handle every dispute with the children knowing she could never afford to put her husband in the position of having to take sides or risk having one of the children set his or her teeth so rabidly against her that her life became unbearable.

She would similarly have to be careful in her use of the word 'family', at least until such time as she had been accepted as part of it by the children themselves. She would need the patience of Job and the wisdom of Solomon, or, at the very least, the continuing support of Mary Jane Kelly.

But, for all that, she had married a reasonably wealthy man and could look forward to a comfortable life with him, something she could only have dreamed about when she was living in a rented flat in the heart of Dublin's red-light district. She would also, it seemed likely, get to see a little of the world, her new husband having a brother and two sons living in Argentina that he was determined to visit at least once before he died.

From the Kellys' point of view, it was one less thing to worry about. The girl would be taken care of, no matter what might happen in the future. And the farm was finally alive with the sound of children. There was comfort in having a younger family close at hand as they faced old age.

PARNELL

THE WEDDING FESTIVITIES concluded; it was straight back to work for William Kelly. He had a conference to attend; a conference of *national* importance.

In a flood of optimism inspired by strong produce

prices during the fifties and sixties, Irish tenant farmers had allowed themselves to be cajoled into paying higher rents. It seemed only fair at the time. High British tariffs on imported grain had given Ireland a privileged and highly profitable access to the British market and this, in turn, had led to increased specialisation in grain production – despite the Irish climate not being particularly suited to the growing of cereals.

Since then, grain prices had plummeted, and Europe had been hit by a period of execrable weather, sodden harvests, and economic depression. A flood of cheap wheat from the United States and Ukraine had forced prices down and rendered Irish grain production uneconomic. In just twenty years, Ireland had gone from being a substantial producer of grain to a country almost completely specialising in beef, dairy, and pig production. The tillage industry was in crisis, but still the landlords refused to reduce rents.

In the midst of this agrarian crisis, a National Land Conference was called for the Rotunda on 20 January 1875 and William Kelly was invited to take the chair. The conference, attended by many of the Tenants Defence associations from around the country, adopted a National Land Bill drafted by Isaac Butt in consultation with the Central Tenants Defence Association, an organisation that was dominated by farmers with large holdings from the east of the country.

The farmers, alas, could not resist constantly tinkering with the bill and making frequent amendments and, as a result, their support of Butt was far from unanimous or unqualified. And yet, despite the burgeoning criticism and growing lack of trust from the membership at large, William Kelly remained steadfastly loyal to his old friend and former barrister, and to the philosophy of peaceful persuasion.

Kelly's chairmanship of this historic conference

more or less confirmed his national profile and influence within the tenants' rights movement. Unlike so many of the other farmers, however, Kelly possessed a natural tone of authority. It had been a prerequisite of his old job. Stewards had to be capable of managing people, and they had to be capable of taking charge. Kelly was no great public speaker, preferring, when the need arose, to express himself in letters. But in the quiet confines of the committee room, he was a clear-thinking, fair-minded, and widely respected colleague.

The conference represented a qualified triumph for Butt and his supporters, but the ground was already shifting beneath their feet. Following Parnell's election, Andrew Kettle, so long a staunch supporter of Butt, slowly began to ally himself ever more closely with the man from Avondale, whose star was very much on the rise. This was not so much an act of estrangement as divergence, for Butt was still highly respected by Kettle as a man.

That sense of waning influence became only too apparent to Kelly at a committee meeting of the County Dublin Tenants Defence Association on the night of Tuesday, 12 May 1875. At this meeting, Kelly, in his role as chairman, requested that Kettle update the committee on the present position regarding the proposed National Land Bill. Kettle spoke briefly, before deferring to Kelly for his opinion. Kelly, who was closer to the tenant farmers than Kettle, more or less confirmed that Butt's bill, in its present form, albeit with some alterations, adequately represented the farmers' case.

Kettle responded cautiously. There had been far too many amendments already. He could 'endorse Mr Kelly's views with regard to the bill,' but he warned that the bill was unlikely to be accepted in its current format by *all* the Home Rule MPs. There simply wasn't enough time left in the current session of parliament to reach a consensus from so broad a miscellany of views and vested interests.

What Kettle meant, of course, was that there wasn't enough time for *Butt* to reach a consensus, on account of his by now famously infrequent attendance at parliament. The diplomatic qualities that Kelly admired in Butt, were coming to be perceived as weaknesses by a general public more appreciative of the obstructionist parliamentary tactics of his colleagues.

After considerable discussion, the committee passed a diplomatically worded resolution regretting the delay in bringing the bill before Parliament and calling on Butt and his colleagues to use their influence to push it forward. They had, after all, been elected on a tenants' rights platform.

A degree of impatience was growing rapidly within the ranks. There were some who doubted that Butt, despite his electoral successes, could *ever* deliver a parliamentary majority by means of peaceful persuasion and, despite his respect for and loyalty to his old friend, William Kelly could sense that Butt was swimming against the tide.

The following October, a meeting of the County Dublin Tenants Defence Association was called to hear from Butt on the latest developments on the land question. It was also attended by Parnell. Before Butt could get to his feet, however, William Kelly was invited to speak, not as a warm-up act for the political heavyweights, but as a respected representative in his own right.

The stout white-haired old gentleman from Portrane gathered his papers and, from amongst a hedge of greybeards, starched collars, and bulging waistcoats, rose slowly to his feet. Reading from a lengthy and pre-prepared statement, he called for fixity of tenure, fair rents, and free sale of goods. He also called, with all the force his raw Monaghan accent could lend to his complaint, for the simplification of leases and the removal of archaic clauses such as the reservation to the lessor of the right of fishing 'where there never was a live fish', or the right of hawking where there are no hawks. He demanded the removal of modern restrictions prohibiting the tenant from selling hay and straw, or clauses compelling him to feed and protect game, as well as a great many other 'injurious and tyrannical clauses.' He went on:

Full justice to the landlord and full justice to the tenants in a short bill, which everyone can understand, and which will leave no loopholes by which clever lawyers will afterwards make it useless, is what we require (hear hear). This we require both for the prosperity and the peace of the country.

When he had finished politely reminding Butt and Parnell of their responsibilities, Kelly then proceeded to lecture the entire assembly on the ancient customs of tanistry and gavelkind in order to illustrate how tenaciously the Irish race had clung to the 'usages of their forefather', and how similar these ancient customs had been to what was now called 'tenants' rights'. They were not just fighting injustice, he suggested, they were re-establishing their culture and racial identity.

It was a powerful, emotional speech, born of years of frustration; an old man approaching the end of his life and pleading to be allowed to see a resolution to the struggle before he died. For perhaps the first time in his life, William Kelly abandoned statistics for passion and, according to the *Freeman's Journal* of the following day, was warmly applauded for his 'very forcible statement'. There was, apparently, life in the old dog yet.

Isaac Butt, when he was eventually called upon, rose to raucous cheers. He spoke at length of the evils of the current laws and the difficulties inherent in getting them changed. He had sat in six parliaments, he said, and of the six this was the one least likely to give a sympathetic hearing to the reforms he was proposing.

At the end of the meeting, after Parnell had spoken briefly, William Kelly, foremost amongst the optimists, proposed a motion of confidence in his old friend's ability to drive the necessary reforms forward in parliament. He did so in the full knowledge that many of those present were nurturing misgivings.

Several newspapers had already been critical of Butt and had placed the blame for the failure of the Irish members to accomplish much at Westminster squarely on his famously frequent absences from parliament. Attacks like this were becoming increasingly proliferate, and more personal, and many of the M.P.s who had been elected on the home rule ticket were now, quite openly, being portrayed as little more than political opportunists.

Kelly's motion was passed, it could hardly have been defeated in the old man's presence, but even those who scarcely knew him could see that the old barrister's health was buckling under the strain of trying to hold so many different factions together. Kettle had already advised Butt that, for the good of his health, he ought to retire. Butt was, however, like William Kelly, a man who had invested far too much of his time and energy in the cause to simply walk away now.

Just two months later, having received a written request from Butt, Kelly put a proposal before the County Dublin Tenants Defence Association, requesting that they be the ones to take the first steps towards the formation of a national body of Tenants Defence associations:

'That the suggestions contained in Mr Butt's letter with reference to the formation of a Central Tenant-right Committee in Dublin to collect information and to keep an accurate record of all cases of landlord oppression, as well as to give the agitation the status it necessarily

demands, is so much in accordance with the views of the association that on referring to our minutes of 1874 we find that resolutions were passed and published advocating this course. We are, therefore, now all the more eager to give Mr Butt's excellent project our best assistance.'

Kelly's motion was seconded by Charles Reilly and, following a show of hands, was duly passed. A further motion led to the formation of this new body and the election to the committee of William Kelly, Maurice Butterly, Edward Hogan, Charles Reilly, James O'Neill, Thomas Grehan, Joseph O'Neill, James F. Grehan, and Andrew Kettle. The new body – to be called the Central Tenants Defence Committee – was thus inaugurated and set on its path with a generous donation of £100 from Patrick Boland.

Kelly's political activities were interrupted a few days later when his good friend, William Nolan of Nethercross, died at his home in The Burrow. He left behind a working farm and five children, two of which had yet to reach their majority.

Back in 1870, Nolan had gone to the offices of James Plunkett and Sons, Solicitors, and drafted his last will and testament. In this document, Nolan had nominated William Kelly of Middlefield and John Davis of The Burrow, not just the executors of his will, but as the guardians of his under-age children. With five children to be considered, Nolan's will was always going to prove complex to execute. In fact, the grant of probate would not be delivered for another two years.

Just two weeks after he had buried his old friend, Kelly travelled up to Dublin for a meeting of the Central Tenant's Defence Committee. Unlike so many other meetings that had taken place at the European Hotel on Bolton Street, this meeting took place at the committee's new offices at 19 Upper Sackville Street. The new railway, opposed by so many in Donabate when it had first been proposed, had at least made the journey tolerable for the old man. He was of an age to remember the hard hours of a journey by horse and carriage. The world was changing, and changing fast, though not always for the worse.

William Kelly was now seventy years of age, Mary Jane seventy-nine, and Nolan's death had served only to remind them of the fact that very soon one of them would most likely be living without the other. With each passing year, their circle of contemporaries had narrowed, and they had come to rely on the broader social contact that William's political activities had afforded them. There was little chance then, of William retiring; in fact, his commitment to his various causes actually increased.

Rather than allowing the indignities of old age to force him from the scene, William Kelly held fast to what was familiar and continued to take on more work than was perhaps good for him. He did not slow down, if anything it was life itself that appeared to have picked up speed, as though it was racing impatiently towards a conclusion.

By now Kelly was serving on the committees of the Central Tenants Defence Committee, the County Dublin Tenants Defence Association, and the Irish National Land League. He was also still serving on the Swords Dispensary Committee and issuing tickets to the poor of his parish for medical care. Every moment was a gift. Enthusiasm, on the other hand, was now fetched with aching limbs from a well that was running steadily dry.

Kelly had recently been installed as chairman of the Central Tenants Defence Committee, but it was far too soon to be expecting progress. The membership was still too Dublin-centred. Nights like this were to be endured rather than savoured, but they were necessary to any cause worth fighting.

This was the dirty work of every revolution, the hard graft of building consensus in smoke-filled rooms, of allowing everyone to speak but no one to dominate or feel excluded. It was the unglamorous side, the routine and tedious side that the great orators often found too menial, but without which they'd never have an audience worth inspiring.

The meeting, as expected, achieved little of consequence apart from an increased sense of camaraderie and a reading from Butt of the latest amendments to his bill. More amendments! Time was slipping by and, for William Kelly, it was becoming increasingly difficult to get excited about projects or stories that he would never live to see concluded. For the first time in his life, he began to leave committee meetings early.

Butt's Land Bill would be discussed in far more detail at a national conference called by the Committee for 15 March. Kelly would attend the conference, not as a member of the Central Committee, but as a delegate of the County Dublin Tenants Defence Association. The county organisation was still closer to his heart. It was populated less by large farmers than by small. He understood these people better, and they him.

Following a slow start, the new Central Tenants Defence Committee, with Kelly and Kettle at the helm, managed to achieve a surprising degree of organisation and common purpose among the various county defence leagues. It even managed to work closely, and largely harmoniously, with Butt.

But it was not to last. That June, in a speech to the House of Commons, Parnell openly defended the action of Fenian rebels in 1867 that had resulted in the accidental killing of a van guard. His popularity in Ireland soared on the back of it and the more moderate Butt began to find himself increasingly marginalised, an old book ready to be filed amongst the political back numbers. Parnell, quite simply, had stolen his thunder.

Kelly, very much a moderate in these matters,

remained an ardent supporter of Butt and, in July 1877, was foremost amongst the subscribers to the 'Butt Testimonial' by members of the County Dublin Tenants Defence Association. In a vain attempt to mirror the annual tribute Irish nationalists had once paid to O'Connell, a fund had been set up by prominent Home Rulers with a view to helping to keep Butt in politics, and in attendance in parliament, rather than seeing him forced to return to his legal career to make ends meet.

Though never enjoying anything like the mass love and loyalty that O'Connell had once inspired, the existence of the fund nevertheless managed to induce Butt to remain at the helm of the Home Rule movement. Kelly had not only been prominent in the fundraising, he had also agreed, despite his many other commitments, to serve on the council of the Home Rule League alongside Butt and Kettle. He would hold this position until at least March 1878. William Kelly was now sitting on the executive committees of ALL the major political movements in the country.

On 21 June 1877, an emergency meeting of the Central Tenants Defence Committee was convened to discuss the Mitchelstown Estate Case (Bridge vs Casey).

This case concerned an action for criminal libel taken by one Patten Smith Bridge, a land agent for Mr Nathaniel Buckley, owner of a remote estate in the Galtee Mountains. The action was taken against a young tenant farmer, John Sarsfield Casey who, earlier that year, had published a letter in the *Freeman's Journal* that Bridge was alleging had attempted to justify his assassination.

The roots of this dispute lay in the decision, in 1851, of the Earl of Kingston to sell a 22,000-acre portion of his estate on the southern slopes of the Galtee Mountains to the aforementioned, Nathaniel

Buckley, an enormously wealthy cotton mill owner from Lancashire. Buckley appointed Bridge to manage his investment, and the latter swiftly began a campaign of intimidation, exorbitant rent increases, and evictions, against the 517 small tenant farmers who resided on his land. Incensed by Bridge's behaviour, Casey had taken up his pen in defence of the tenants.

On that bright June morning in 1877, an open letter from E.D. Gray M.P to Isaac Butt was published in the *Freeman's Journal* stating that Casey's trial was due to begin in two days time and that, in order to secure a fair trial for Casey, it would be necessary to bring a large number of witnesses from remote places such as Ballyporeen, Clogheen, and Mitchelstown. This would not be possible, he wrote, unless funds could be raised through public subscription. With this in mind, Gray had opened a subscription list through the medium of the *Freeman's Journal*, and an account in the National Bank to which he himself had donated the sum of £25.

At a hastily-convened meeting of the Central Tenants Defence Committee, those present unanimously decided to support the fund. William Kelly personally donated the sum of £1. He would make a further donation of £2 on 17 December though this time it would be in a personal capacity rather than as a member of the Committee. The plight of John Sarsfield Casey had touched something in William Kelly that went deeper than the usual tenants' rights issue.

Despite the objections of the trial judge, Casey was acquitted when, after an eight-day trial in which Casey was represented by Kelly's old barrister, Isaac Butt, the jury could not agree on a verdict. The trial, followed widely at home and abroad, highlighted the plight of small tenant farmers and helped the various Tenants Right organisations to harvest further support for their cause.

The potato crop failed again in 1877 and the feeling abroad was that another catastrophe was in the offing. Most believed that it would only affect the western counties. It came as a shock when the south and east of the country were also affected.

At a meeting of the Central Tenants Defence Committee, on Wednesday, 28 November 1877, William Kelly tendered a motion calling for a meeting of all the tenant bodies in Ireland to decide the best means of advancing the cause of land reform during the next session of parliament. The motion was passed and the meeting was scheduled to take place in Dublin on 18 December.

At this meeting, Kelly once again took the chair. The meeting, however, was poorly attended, primarily due to its proximity to the Home Rule Conference, which many other delegates had wanted to attend. Attendance was also negatively affected by a recent spell of bad weather that had seen rivers frozen to a depth of three inches and heavy snowfall blocking the mountain passes. Kelly's agenda, as a result, was effectively postponed.

In the meantime, and despite his advanced age and multiple political commitments, Kelly took on yet more responsibilities with the Balrothery Poor Law Union when he allowed himself to be elected to a committee to oversee the implementation in his district of the Contagious Diseases (Animals) Act 1878. This act dealt with the slaughter of infected cattle and the payment of compensation to farmers from the General Cattle Diseases Fund. It also dealt with public health issues such as the registration of all persons carrying on the trade of cow keepers, dairymen, or purveyors of milk and the certification of hygiene standards in the dairy industry to prevent the sale of infected or contaminated milk.

In its early days at least, this committee would have been extremely busy, but Kelly still continued to chair meetings of the Central Tenants Defence Committee and to attend meetings of the Swords District Dispensary Committee. He was very much the local 'councillor' now, making sure that his constituents did not lose out through lack of representation, while at the same time pursuing his own agenda at a national level.

None of this could ever have been possible without Mary Jane's support. The wife of such a man as William Kelly, a man with his fingers in so many different political pies, would have had to have had her own skills in order to promote her husband and ease his way in the world. She would have required charm and authority, and a memory for names and faces that rivalled her parish priest. She would have had to have been as devoted to the causes he espoused as he was. To have been otherwise would have been to undermine his credibility.

But she was eighty-one years of age now, and though her health was beginning to fail, her husband remained reluctant to pass the baton to a younger man. Their front door continued to welcome a steady stream of the importunate poor coming to plead for dispensary tickets, not to mention important members of the Home Rule Party and various tenants' rights movements. Having so many meetings to attend in Dublin, her husband was frequently absent from home and Mary Jane would frequently be left alone to deal with callers. As a result, she would have been as familiar a face to the poor of the parish as William Kelly himself. She, too, had had her part to play in the fight.

But had that fight already been lost? On 4 May 1878, the *Irish Times* carried an advertisement for an auction of farm goods to be held at Portrane House five days later. The auction had been occasioned by the seizure of goods following the 'non-payment of rent'. Taken alongside the fact that the grasslands of Portrane Demesne were by now being leased on an *annual basis*, and leases granted on foot of a competitive auction, we can perhaps glean some idea of the challenges and insecurities facing the tenant farmers of Portrane at this time.

Amongst the goods to be auctioned were over thirty head of well-bred cattle, horses, carriages, harnesses, fifty tons of hay, greenhouse plants, and excellent bed-chamber furniture. There is nothing in the advert to suggest that any of the property or goods to be auctioned belonged to William Kelly, but whoever they did belong to must at one stage have been, like Kelly, a prosperous tenant farmer of the Evans Estate.

The social and topographical landscape of the peninsula was slowly becoming unrecognisable and the Kellys could hardly have been left unaffected. If they were fighting for anything now, it was principles. The land had almost certainly gone.

If William Kelly had had no hand, act, or part in that first auction, he most certainly had in the next. On 9 August 1878, following the grant of probate, the chattels of the late William Nolan were finally auctioned in The Burrow of Portrane. As one of the executors of Nolan's will, Kelly would have been heavily involved. So many of his old friends and neighbours had gone now. The community that had once fit him like a glove, was slowly becoming threadbare and cold.

Within days of William Nolan's farm being auctioned, the increasingly popular and more radical Parnell finally replaced Butt as president of the Home Rule Confederation of Great Britain. Buoyed by his success, he began to negotiate with leading Fenians and several tenant defence associations with a view to producing a political alliance and a joint strategy.

Isaac Butt had become so marginalised by now that on one occasion the son of one of his dearest friends, the newspaper magnate, A.M. O'Sullivan, refused to shake his hand and called him a 'damned

Englishman'. He died, a broken man, on 5 May 1879, his great brain, as Andrew Kettle would later write, having finally given way 'under the terrible strain of overwork'.

It seemed that the way was finally clear for Parnell to become the leader of the Irish Home Rule Party. The moderate majority, however, held sway and voted in William Shaw as chairman. This was not something that William Kelly would have welcomed as Shaw was famously opposed to the Land League, the primary reason for Kelly's involvement in the Home Rule movement.

In fact, at least in Ireland, Shaw was probably better known for being the chairman of the Munster Bank than for any forcibly held political opinion on either the land *or* national questions. With his old friend Isaac Butt gone, and Shaw now at the helm, Kelly's involvement in the Home Rule Party steadily diminished.

Parnell, rapidly growing in stature and improving as a public speaker, responded to Shaw's election by moving further from a moderate position to a far more radical stance. He even went so far as to exhort an assembled crowd in Westport on 8 June to 'keep a firm grip on your homesteads and lands', coming as close as he dared in the current climate to advocating something more than passive resistance. If it came to a choice between Shaw and Parnell, William Kelly now knew, without a shadow of a doubt, to which mast he would nail his colours.

By September, the continuous rain had destroyed the summer crops and fears of another famine escalated into certainty. In Dublin, the Castle continued to deny what was staring the rest of the country in the face. The rumours, they claimed, were the invention of 'mercenary and disloyal agitators.' But beyond the Pale the blight in the fields could be neither disguised nor dismissed.

That December, William Kelly was invited to judge

the ‘roots’ Category at the RDS Christmas Show. It was to be his final visit; the last time that anyone would remember him for the great agriculturist he had once been. Though not yet gone, William Kelly was already on his way to being forgotten.

THE LAND LEAGUE

BY 1879, THE potato crop had failed for three years running, small tenant farmers had become so impoverished they had to choose between paying their rents or feeding their families. Evictions were once again on the rise.

Across the country secret societies began to take violent action against landlords and their agents. The police, encouraged by the suspension of the Habeus Corpus Act, responded by arresting 'the usual suspects' and detaining them without charge. The inevitable happened.

Spurred into action by the increasing number of evictions, a certain Michael Davitt began to organise a movement of resistance. On 20 April 1879, he helped to arrange a large 'Tenant Right' meeting at Irishtown, Co. Mayo. It was attended by between seven and thirteen thousand people, *despite* the opposition of the Catholic hierarchy. Newspapers reported it as the largest public meeting in the country since the 'monster' meetings of O'Connell. Davitt himself, however, did not speak. He was still on parole following his release from prison.

Ireland had seen large-scale protest meetings before in which deferential and conciliatory appeals had been made to landlords or government for rent relief or land reform. This meeting was very different. For a start, it brought together a more diverse audience than had ever been seen at such meetings before, from country dwellers to townspeople, small to large farmers, Fenians to Constitutionalists.

It was also very different in tone, giving voice to nationalist, militant and retributive ideas that would in a short space of time give rise to the demand for the abolition of the landlord system altogether. The landlords were portrayed as avaricious, violating God's intention for the land by exploiting both it and the people who worked it. The most common call from the platform was for the non-payment of exorbitantly high rents.

Out of this meeting, and the repeat performances that followed, was born the Land League of Mayo, which shortly afterwards enjoyed its first real success in a campaign against a landowning Catholic priest who was threatening his tenants with eviction. The very fact that the League would go after a Catholic priest was indicative, not just of the current degree of rural distress, but of a murmuring tide of militancy that would force numerous Catholic priests and bishops into joining the movement for fear of losing their positions of authority to others.

Davitt's background was more industrial than agricultural. Born in Mayo, he had emigrated to Lancashire to find work, had lost an arm in a mill accident at the age of eleven, and had been imprisoned for gun-running at the age of twenty-four. He brought to Irish politics, and to the tenants' rights movement in particular, the zeal and tactics of a trade unionist.

The rent strike Davitt organised against Fr. Ulick

Burke, not only prevented an eviction and secured for the beleaguered tenant a 25% reduction in his rent, it proved to be a high profile and spectacular success that more or less marked the beginning of what would later be called 'The Land War'.

Later that year, Parnell was approached by Davitt and urged to help him formally join the Land League of Mayo to a national body. In so doing Davitt initiated one of the most remarkable working partnerships in Irish history. On the face of it, the two had little in common. Parnell was a conservative capitalist and Davitt a reactionary socialist, but they found common ground in a shared nationalism and a deep personal hatred of Britain – Parnell's inherited from his American mother and Davitt's from the many years he spent as a Fenian prisoner in Dartmoor prison, much of it in solitary confinement.

Parnell agreed to Davitt's suggestion on condition that the platform to be put forward should be a parliamentary one capable of being as freely expressed in the House of Commons as on the streets of Ireland. He also insisted on the absorption of men like William Kelly into the executive of the new national organization because 'the men in America would not have confidence in the new land movement unless the leading tenant right men would join.'

On 12 June 1879, a special general meeting of the Central Tenants Defence Committee was convened at the European Hotel in Dublin and once again William Kelly took the chair. The meeting resolved to send a deputation to London to represent the movement at the forthcoming land conference. They also resolved to change the name of the association to the Tenants' Central Association of Ireland and to lower the annual subscription to ten shillings. It would appear that the movement was, if not exactly struggling, then at least suffering from a degree of inertia and badly in need of new blood and new ideas.

Michael Davitt

In response to a circular issued by Charles Stewart Parnell, a meeting was called for 2 p.m. on Tuesday, 21 October 1879 to inaugurate a new *national* Land League. The meeting took place at the Imperial Hotel on Dublin's Sackville Street (more latterly Clery's Department Store) and was presided over by Andrew Kettle, secretary of the newly rebranded and soon to be defunct Tenants' Central Association of Ireland.

The first resolution on the conference agenda was to name the new association. Proposed by the Rev. Father Behan, C.C, and seconded Mr William Dillon, B.L. It read:

'That an association be hereby formed to be named the Irish National Land League.'

The second resolution, dealing with the purpose of the new organisation, was proposed by William Kelly and seconded by Thomas Roe:

'That the objects of the league are: First, to bring about a reduction of rack-rents; second, to facilitate the obtaining of the ownership of the soil by the occupiers.'

These objectives were to be attained by;

'...promoting organization among tenant farmers; by defending those who may be threatened with eviction for refusing to pay unjust rents; by facilitating the working of the Bright clauses of the Land act during the winter; and by obtaining such a reform in the laws relating to land as will enable every tenant to become the owner of his holding by paying a fair rent for a limited number of years'

The above statement more or less encapsulated the Land League's vision of a modern Ireland, of a country where every tenant could become the owner of his holding. This vision would be further underscored in an address to the Farmers of Ireland by Michael Davitt that was printed on 5 November and subsequently published in the Dublin and regional newspapers. The address was accompanied by a plea to supporters to keep sectarian politics out of a campaign that was intended to benefit Catholics and Protestants alike.

Following the formation of the new organisation, Parnell was elected president and William Kelly was appointed, as expected, to the Executive Committee. Attention now turned to the details of the new party's parliamentary campaign. In order to form a manifesto, and receive a democratic mandate to follow it, it was decided to call a national convention. It was fixed to meet at the Rotunda Hospital, on 29 April of the following year.

A sub-committee was formed to handle the work of preparing a manifesto to be laid before the assembly of delegates for their approval. It comprised of just five men: Charles Stewart Parnell, Patrick Egan, Andrew Kettle, James J. Louden, and William Kelly. This was, arguably, one of the pivotal moments in the creation of the modern Irish state and William Kelly was once again at the heart of it.

The manifesto of the newly formed Irish National Land League was finalised during an all-night session of negotiation and debate on the eve of the conference at Morrison's Hotel at the corner of Dawson Street and Nassau Street (opposite the entrance to Trinity College). This historic document was signed by all five of the men who drafted it and would, in time, provide the template for all subsequent land purchase schemes proposed for Ireland by successive British governments. In many respects, it is probably as important and influential a document to the birth of the Irish Nation as the Proclamation of Independence.

There should, of course, have been six signatures, and one name was conspicuous by its absence. Michael Davitt, who had attended the meeting and was present throughout the protracted and difficult negotiations, refused to sign. 'The price offered to the landlords,' he protested, 'was too high'. In Davitt's mind, the proposal ignored the value of a tenant's improvements to his property and the expected fall of agricultural prices due to the expected increase in external competition.

Those aspects of the compromise that so concerned Davitt, would once also have concerned William Kelly, who had suffered personal loss on foot of the existing legislation on these matters. But Kelly, like all farmers, was a pragmatist. He understood that some battles were worth losing in order to win the war. The real prize was the land. The focus had to be kept on that. The land *had* to belong to those who worked it. The evictions had to be stopped.

That December, Parnell and John Dillon travelled to the US to raise funds for the Land League and to address the American House of Representatives. While they were gone, parliament was unexpectedly dissolved, forcing Parnell to return home to fight an election.

The following April, Parnell was elected for Mayo, Meath, and Cork, and chose to sit for the latter. On 17 May, he moved against William Shaw, who was still chairman of the Irish Home Rule Party, defeating him by 23 votes to 18. The moderates were left shaken and despondent. Control of the movement had passed to a younger, more radical, and more militant generation. It was time, or so it must have seemed at the time, for the old guard to vacate the stage.

By this point, William Kelly had largely withdrawn from active engagement in the Home Rule Movement, in favour of greater involvement with the Irish National Land League, where he continued to work alongside Davitt and Kettle on the national committee. His attendance at the weekly meetings of the committee is quite consistent between January and April, and on both 27 February and 6 March various organs of the national press record him as actually chairing those meetings, meetings that were becoming increasingly radical in tone.

The first tactic employed by the new Land League was to establish a form of collective bargaining that would impose an economic imperative on landlords to lower their rents. This involved the boycotting of any person who dared to take over the farm of an evicted farmer. The increasingly militant Kettle, however, went further and urged tenants who believed they were being charged excessive rents to pay only 'at the point of a bayonet.'

Peaceful intimidation moved swiftly beyond mere boycotts and rent strikes and deteriorated into such violence that the campaign came to be known as 'The Land War'. The number of agrarian outrages grew from 863 incidents in 1879 to 2,590 in 1880, following an increase in evictions during the same period from 1,238 to 2,110. Among the landlords to lose their lives were Lords Mountmorris and Leitrim.

Parnell, opposed to acts of violence, took a leaf out of O'Connell's book of political stratagems and sought to replace violent agitation with monster meetings. He also sought to encourage a wider application of Davitt's 'boycott' tactics. In combination, he believed, these essentially peaceful tactics would put enough pressure on Gladstone to ensure the passage of a home rule bill.

In the end, it was the increasing tempo of agrarian violence as much as Parnell's increasingly separatist tone, that eventually forced Gladstone's hand. Yielding to the advice of his cabinet that if land reform was not preceded by some form of sanction against those who participated in, or actively supported, acts of violence, he would be seen to be rewarding such acts, he introduced, in January 1881, a Protection of Persons and Property Bill. Popularly called the Coercion Bill, it authorized the internment without trial of any person suspected of involvement in the 'Land War'.

Outraged Irish MPs responded with a campaign of filibustering that proved so effective it completely tied up the business of the House of Commons for over seven weeks. An exasperated government was left with little option but to 'set aside' normal procedure and force through an amendment to the rules to allow for guillotine motions. An infuriated Parnell had to be forcibly removed from the house.

Face saved, Gladstone now attempted to defuse the Irish situation and neutralize the more violent wings of the Land League. He did this by introducing a Land Act that prevented the eviction of tenants whose rent was not in arrears and established a Land Court and Land Commission to arbitrate on the 'fairness' of rents. It took fifty-eight sittings of parliament but, eventually, the bill was enacted.

Real progress was finally being made on the land issue, but it was not enough to satisfy the Irish

National Land League. It had not, they insisted, gone far enough to meet their demands of 'the three Fs', nor had it offered rent reductions or an amnesty for arrears. William Kelly was left similarly unenthused, and no longer felt able to make the considerable effort it now took to travel from his home at Middlefield to weekly committee meetings in Dublin.

Age had finally caught up with William Kelly. Both he and his wife were in failing health, the latter so seriously ill that she required constant attendance, the kindest solicitude, and a deal of palliative care. Kelly's involvement in the Land League, in consequence, now became sporadic at best.

BACK TO THE GARDEN

THE FIRST BLOSSOMS of blackthorn had barely graced the hedgerows, filling the countryside with the promise of new life, when Mary Jane Kelly took her last earthly breath. She was eighty-four.

It was Tuesday, 8 March 1881, and Mary Jane had finally succumbed to what was described on her death certificate as 'congestion of the lung' – a condition that at her advanced age is unlikely to have assailed her suddenly and was most probably related to an underlying cardiac condition.

Her funeral mass took place the following Thursday at Middlefield House, after which the cortege of carriages set off on the twelve-mile journey to Prospect Cemetery in Glasnevin. Here, in the plot that William had purchased for them some twenty-one years previous, Mary Jane Kelly was laid to rest alongside her beloved brother James (who may possibly have been her twin), and also her niece, Mary Jane. The burial was registered by Mary Jane Derrick's husband, John McAllister, at that time still resident at Middlefield.

Today the Shanks' grave lies bereft of a headstone. If it ever *had* been marked, then it was most likely with a plain wooden cross that has probably long since rotted away. William Kelly may once have intended to erect a more permanent memorial to his dearly departed wife, but nothing was ever done about it: it was, after all, the Shanks' family plot now, and not his own. In any case, his own health was now failing.

Having followed the coffin of his life's companion to Glasnevin, William Kelly returned that evening to Middlefield and a house redolent of candle wax, swinging censers, and the quiet realisation that the next funeral he was likely to attend would be his own. For at least a year prior to his wife's passing, he had been surviving on a borrowed vitality, energised by a political campaign that, newly radicalised, had at last appeared to be gathering real momentum.

But all sorts of things expire upon the passing of a spouse. He had devoted the latter years of his life to a woman and a cause that no longer needed him. He had lived to see a younger generation take control of a struggle that had for so long been his reason to get up in the mornings. But what was he to do now? What did any of it matter now?

A month after his wife's death Kelly managed to rouse himself sufficiently from the gloom to attend a meeting of the national committee of the Land League, but having made the effort once, he then failed to turn up for the Land Conference at the end of that same month, or to attend any other meetings during the following two. He next appeared on 23 July, attended a further two meetings on 17 and 24 August but, after that, he appears to have withdrawn from public life completely. The fight had gone from William Kelly and, without Mary Jane by his side, his health declined rapidly.

Autumn came. The days drew in and the last of the swallows left for the long journey south. The apples had long since been collected and barrelled and the crops, such as they were, had all been harvested. At Middlefield, the arrival of the cold weather brought with it the sense of an ending.

On 13 October 1881, Charles Stewart Parnell was arrested under the Coercion Act on foot of a newspaper article that had allegedly sought to incite acts of intimidation and non-payment of rent. News of his arrest was met with amazement and alarm and such was the expectation of a violent backlash that, as Parnell was being ferried from Morrison's Hotel to the city centre, he would pass a force of no less than one hundred policemen, the majority of whom had mustered in Foster Place, ready to deal firmly with protesters.

Politically, the arrest could not have come at a better time for Parnell. The Land League had fragmented following the passing of Gladstone's Land Act and the martyrdom of its leading lights would either give fresh impetus to the movement or crush it completely. Parnell was determined that it should be the former.

Over subsequent days, several other leading figures in the Land League would also be arrested and imprisoned and protesting crowds would be baton-charged and beaten. Had William Kelly still been in reasonable health, he might well have been amongst their number and his name would most probably have passed into the pantheon of nationalist heroes along with the rest of them. But, somewhat ironically, death contrived to rob William Kelly of the 'martyrdom' that made so many of his former colleagues' political reputations.

William Kelly was not in Dublin at the time of the arrests, because he was lying at home in Middlefield in seriously failing health. A frail shadow of the man he had once been, he died, just three days after Parnell's arrest, at the fine Georgian farmhouse he'd built for Mary Jane at Middlefield – a landmark building that can still be seen today standing proudly atop a piece of rising ground to the north of the Portrane Road. The death was registered by Elizabeth McGorish.

Like William Kelly, Elizabeth McGorish had been

born in Monaghan, and it is highly probable that she was, in some way or other, related to him. Her brother, Owen, would return to Monaghan shortly after the funeral, but Elizabeth would never leave Middlefield House. Before the following summer had ended, she would have married John McAllister's younger brother, and her children and their descendants would continue to live at Middlefield House until the early 1950s.

William's cause of death was listed simply as 'natural decline of life' and he was buried, not alongside his wife, but with his mother, in the Garden Section of Prospect Cemetery in Glasnevin. He was buried with his own family, such as it was, just as Mary Jane had been buried with hers, most probably because he and Mary Jane did not have any children to warrant the cost of a family grave. Owen McGorish registered the burial.

Surprisingly, for someone who had done so much for both his community and the cause of tenants' rights, William Kelly's death was not marked by even a small obituary in the Dublin press. Many of his former colleagues were in prison at the time, while others were lying low, waiting for the dreaded knock on the door. In any case, Kelly had been largely absent from their lives for the best part of a year and would not really have been as close to the younger generation of radicals that had taken control of the struggle as he had once been to the older generation.

Still, not even his old ally, Edward Purdon, a man who had been so fulsome in his public praise of Kelly in the past and was, at this stage of his life, a former Lord Mayor of Dublin, would put pen to paper to mark old Kelly's passing. This, too, perhaps, may have been rooted in a fear of falling foul of the Coercion Act, for just two days after Kelly's funeral the Land League would be declared an illegal organisation. One could hardly write the obituary of one of its leading lights without mentioning, or at least alluding, to either the

organisation in which he had most recently served, or the tenants' rights movements of the seventies. The monument that stands over his grave, was similarly dedicated without any mention of such service.

William Kelly never lived to see the cause for which he had fought so long finally come to fruition in a progressive series of legislation that culminated in the Wyndham Act of 1903. Thirty years after that, thanks to committed activists like him, fifteen of the country's seventeen million acres of leased land would have been bought out by tenants. A mere half a century after William Kelly's death the confiscations would have been reversed; the land question finally resolved, and Irish agriculture dragged into the scientific age. But William Kelly, and his part in all of that, would be entirely forgotten. In politics, as in show business, timing is everything.

Kelly left behind effects to a value of £1,064 – a considerable sum for those days – and the executors of his will were named as Maurice Butterly of Blanchardstown and Thomas McCourt of Lanestown in Donabate. Both were described as 'farmers', but they had been very much more than that. They had been close friends of Kelly's and political comrades-in-arms from the tenants' rights campaigns of the 1870s .

Kelly's assets were distributed on 12 January 1882. Details of the will were, unfortunately, incinerated during the civil war of 1922, but subsequent ownership would appear to suggest that the was left to either John and Mary Jane McAllister, or to Elizabeth McGorish, who married John's third son, Charlie, on 22 June of that year.

Sometime after William's death, an austere granite obelisk, crafted in the Egyptian revivalist style of the Victorian period, was commissioned by his friends. It paid solemn tribute to a couple who had been 'respected by the poor and esteemed by their many friends and acquaintances'. To this day it remains the only memorial to William Kelly. On the Portrane peninsula, the few that still recognise the name, know him only as Mrs Evans' steward; a brief footnote in the history of the local landed gentry.

A CURIOUS EXHUMATION

LAID TO REST. Eternal rest. Resting in peace. The most common euphemisms for burial have about them the not unreasonable suggestion of permanency. A person's grave, after all, is still generally referred to as their *final* resting place, the *last* remove. In the case of Mary Jane Kelly, however, nothing could have been further from the truth.

The monument to William Kelly still stands in Glasnevin Cemetery, shaded by overhanging yew trees and artfully concealing a scandal. His wife, Mary Jane, is tactfully remembered on the monument that stands upon his grave, but her mortal remains are neither interred within it nor do they reside any longer within the grave into which she had initially been 'laid to rest' just seven months prior to her beloved husband's demise.

Orders for exhumations were not granted lightly, even in 19th century Ireland. There were the obvious public health concerns to be overcome, not to mention the basic moral premise that the dead should be allowed to 'rest in peace'. Indeed, the recently enacted offence of 'disturbing a burial' was largely based on the Victorian value that every human burial should be for eternity.

And so, on Tuesday, 10 April 1883, when Mary Jane Kelly's remains were exhumed from a grave that had already been bought and paid for by her husband, and in which her brother and favourite niece already lay buried, there must have been an extremely compelling reason. That they should then be removed to an unmarked pauper's plot (photo above) in the northeast corner of the Glasnevin Cemetery when her husband was buried less than 100m away, is almost beyond comprehension.

NAMES	AGES					RESIDENCES	MARK OF GRAVE	
	ADULTS	CHILDREN						
	Years	Years	Months	Weeks	Days		Latitude	Longitude
Mary Jane Kelly	84					Portrane Donabate County Dublin	M	71
	Removed per order 1194. 10th April 1883						F	

All that is known for certain of this curious episode, is that the exhumation and re-internment were carried out on foot of an official request marked as 'Order no. 1194'. Under this reference number, the minute books of the Dublin Cemeteries Committee note only that this exhumation had been requested, and that permission had been granted. They do not provide any explanation or reason for the request, or for the subsequent decision. As the letter requesting the exhumation no longer exists, an explanation may never be found.

The only people who could reasonably have requested such an exhumation and reburial, however, were the executors of William Kelly's will, the Shanks family themselves, or some religious authority making a petition under ecclesiastical law. But it seems unlikely, does it not, that the executors who had just erected a monument to her husband, the epitaph on which began 'sacred to the memory of Mrs M.J. Kelly, the beloved wife of William Kelly of Middlefield, Donabate,' could have ordered such a hateful thing just two years after her death.

What appears even more astonishing in this inexplicable affair, is the fact that Mary Jane McAllister was still alive at the time, and was a Shanks by birth. And yet, despite this, the exhumation was allowed to proceed unhindered. Why didn't she put a stop to it? She had, after all, so many reasons to be grateful to the Kellys.

On the cold, hard facts, at least as they are currently known, the episode appears suggestive of an act of retribution. But over what? Had the Shanks family felt aggrieved over some aspect of William Kelly's will? Had some hideous mix-up occurred at the time the monument was being raised on William Kelly's grave? Or was it simply the bitterness of a family that felt that one of their own had abandoned them; had gone to live in a big house with spare rooms when they had been abandoned to the slums?

All we can know for certain is that, under Section 170 of the Public Health Act of 1878, it had become illegal for someone to be buried in a family grave without the expressed permission of the relatives of those already interred:

'Where by usage or otherwise any grave vault or place of internment in any burial ground or cemetery

has been the burying place of and used as such by any family, no corpse of any person not having been a member of such family shall be buried in such grave vault or place of interment without the consent in writing of some immediate relative of the member of such family last interred therein; and if any person shall knowingly act or assist in any burial contrary to the provisions of this section, every such person shall be liable, on summary conviction before a court of summary jurisdiction, to a penalty not exceeding ten pounds; and upon any complaint made under this section it shall be lawful for the court to make such order for the exhumation and re-interment of such corpse so buried as to such court shall seem fit.'

So, had someone within the extended Shanks family complained? And if they had, then who exactly could they have been, and why would they do such a thing? Had William Kelly, despite having paid for the Shanks family grave in the first place, forgotten or deliberately neglected to seek the permission of the wider family when he buried his wife? And if so, why? What could he possibly have been afraid of?

Was this simply a matter of old age, crippling grief, or long-held grudges? Or, could it possibly be the case that Mary Jane Kelly had been reburied in a paupers' grave simply because the Shanks family could not obtain permission to re-inter her alongside William Kelly, there being no family left on his side capable of granting permission?

On the face of it, this would appear to be a reasonable enough explanation. But even if that *was* the case, and Elizabeth McGorish had *not* been a blood relative, it would hardly explain the exhumation. Why would they go the trouble of exhuming the body in the first place if they had not already gotten permission to re-inter it somewhere else? It all seems too deliberate to have been a simple misunderstanding.

Whatever the reason for Mary Jane Kelly's

exhumation may have been, it was hardly in keeping with an epitaph of 'respected by the poor.' A grave without a headstone. A hero without a memorial. It seems poor reward for two ordinary lives of extraordinary public service.

Sic transit gloria mundi.

Bibliography

Illustrations

Index

SELECT BIBLIOGRAPHY

Agricultural Journal and Transactions of the Lower Canada Agricultural Society, The Society, Montreal, January 1848, January 1849 and June 1849.

Abuse of the Irish Medical Dispensaries, The Lancet, Vol. 153, Issue 3933, p122-124, January 14th, 1899.

Brunt, Liam, and Edmund Cannon. "The Irish Grain Trade from the Famine to the First World War." The Economic History Review, vol. 57, no. 1, 2004, pp. 33–79. JSTOR, www.jstor.org/stable/3698666.

Burke, Helen. *'The People and the Poor Law in 19th Century Ireland'.* Women's Education Bureau, Dublin, 1987.

Calendar of Wills and Administrations, Irish National Archives Digital Collections, Wills and Administrations 1881, p336.

Casey, Brian. *Class and Community in Provincial Ireland, 1851–1914*, Springer, 2018.

Cassell, Ronald Drake. 'Medical Charities, Medical Politics: The Irish Dispensary System and the Poor Law, 1836-1872', Boydell & Brewer Ltd, 1997.

Clapperton, James. *Instructions for the Small Farmers of Ireland, on the cropping and culture of their farms, etc.* W. Curry, Jun., & Company, 1847

Cobbe, Frances Power. *Life of Frances Power Cobbe*, Houghton, Boston 1894.

Collins, Sinéad. *Balrothery Poor Law Union, County Dublin, 1839-1851*, Four Courts Press, Dublin, 2005.

Cox, C. & Luddy, M. *Cultures of Care in Irish Medical History 1750-1970*, Springer, 2010.

Curry, William. Irish Farmer's and Gardener's Magazine and Register of Rural Affairs, Volume 2, June, 1835.

Davitt, Michael. *The Fall of Feudalism in Ireland. Or. The Story of The Land League Revolution.* 1904

Deputy Keeper of Ireland, Index to the Act or Grant Books, and to Original Wills, of the Diocese of Dublin 1272-1858 (26th, 30th and 31st Reports, 1894, 1899), p428.

Digwell, Philip. *Modern Agriculture, as peculiarly applicable to Ireland,* James McGlashan; P. D. Hardy & Sons, 1848.

Doyle, Martin (pseud. [i.e. William Hickey]). *Hints for the Small Farmers of Ireland.* 4th ed. J. Charles, 1830 - 175 pages

Doyle, Martin (pseud. [i.e. William Hickey]). *On Agricultural Schools,* in Irish Farmer's and Gardener's Magazine, Vol.1, June 1834.

Doyle, P.A. *Bannow School,* The Past: The Organ of the Uí Cinsealaigh Historical Society, No.1, Nov. 1920, pp. 122-128

Dublin Irish Famine Mapping Tool, All-Ireland Research Observatory (AIRO), Maynooth University. http://airo.maynoothuniversity.ie/external-content/famine-mapping-1841-1851-county-dublin

Fitzpatrick, H. *Ireland's Grievance, political and statistical. To which is added Mr Scully's Statement of the Penal Laws*: published first in 1812, by H. Fitzpatrick. [Being "Tracts on Ireland, political and statistical. No. 1-6."], Ireland, 1824.

Fogarty, Chris. *The Mass Graves of Ireland: 1845-1850,* Oct. 26 and Nov. 2, 1996, The Irish People, NYC.

Fullarton, A: The Parliamentary Gazetteer of Ireland: Adapted to the New Poor-law, Franchise, Municipal and Ecclesiastical Arrangements; Vol 1, Dublin 1846.

Freeman, Thomas Walter. *Pre-famine Ireland: A Study in Historical Geography,* Manchester University Press, 1957.

Grace, Maria. *Land Stewards: Professional help in running an estate*, English History Authors Blogspot, 19/02/2019, https://englishhistoryauthors.blogspot.com/2017/11/land-stewards-professional-help-in.html

Holland, John J. *The Bannow Farm School (1821-1827)*, Browne & Nolan Ltd., Dublin, 1932.

Kane, A. *Constructing Irish National Identity: Discourse and Ritual during the Land War, 1879–1882*, Springer, 2011.

Kelly, William (steward), *An essay on the general management of villa farms, the manures attainable and applicable to such farms : also, a mode of cultivating two acres of ground, whereby eight cows can be fed throughout the year : with some remarks on the management of small farms in general'*, J. Porter Dublin 1836.

Kelly, William. *The crops proper to be grown at this emergency, and their culture*, Leinster Express, Dec. 12th 1846; p4.

Kelly, William, *'The Irish Small Farmer of 1847; Containing Ample Directions for the Cultivation of the Soil During the Present Crisis*, Cumming & Ferguson, 1847.

Kettle, Andrew J. *The material for victory / being the memoirs of A.J. Kettle. Edited with an introduction, biographical note and appendix by L.J. Kettle*, Fallon, Dublin, 1958.

Lyons, Mary. *The Memoirs of Mrs Leeson, Madam.* Lilliput Press, Dublin, 1995.

Maxwell, Ian. *Everyday Life in 19th Century Ireland.* The History Press, November 2012.

McCabe, Graham. *Patrick McCabe.* Family Genealogy. https://www.irelandxo.com/sites/default/files/AA%20Intro%20and%20Patrick%201840-1913.pdf

McCaffrey, Lawrence J. “Home Rule and the General Election of 1874 in Ireland.” Irish Historical Studies, vol. 9, no. 34, 1954, pp. 190–212. JSTOR, www.jstor.org/stable/30005687.

McCaffrey, Lawrence J. “The Home Rule Party and Irish Nationalist Opinion, 1874-1876.” The Catholic Historical Review, vol. 43, no. 2, 1957, pp. 160–177. JSTOR, www.jstor.org/stable/25016191.

‘*Meeting of the Guardians of Athy Union*’, Leinster Express, August 21st 1841, p3.

Moran, Gerard. *The Land War, Urban Destitution and Town Tenant Protest, 1879-1882.* Saothar, Vol. 20, 1995, pp. 17–30. JSTOR, www.jstor.org/stable/23197221.

O’ Connor. J. *The Workhouses of Ireland: The Fate of Ireland’s Poor,* Anvil Books, Dublin, 1995.

Ó Gráda, Cormac. *Ireland’s Great Famine: An Overview*, University College Dublin, WP04/25, November 2004

Ó Gráda, Cormac. *The lumper potato and the famine*, in ‘The Great Famine – Irish Perspectives’, Pen & Sword, 2018.

O’Keeffe, Tadgh and Ryan, Patrick. *At the World’s End: The Lost Landscape of Monto, Dublin’s Notorious Red-light District*, Landscapes, I, 21-38, 2009.

Ó’Mearáin, Lorcan. “Estate Agents in Farney: Trench & Mitchell.” Clogher Record, vol. 10, no. 3, 1981, pp. 405–413. JSTOR, www.jstor.org/stable/27695836

Papers Relative to the Agricultural School at Bannow, Ordered, by The House of Commons, to be printed, 1 April 1824. University of Southampton Library Digitisation Unit.

Schimmel, Gordon L. ‘*Education through manual labor: a comparative study of selected self-help schools in the United States and Africa.*’, University of Massachusetts Amherst, 1973.

Smyth, Hazel P. *Two Hundred Years a'Growing: The Story of Mackey's Seeds Limited — 1777-1977*, Dublin Historical Record, Vol. 35, No. 3 (Jun., 1982), pp. 100-115 (19 pages)

Sullivan, Thomas. 'On the Cultivation of Wheat'. British Farmer's Magazine, Issue 11, James Ridgway, 1847.

'The Dublin Almanac and General Register of Ireland for the Year of Our Lord, 1842', Pettigrew & Oulton, Dublin 1842.
'*The Potato*'. Tuam Herald, Aug. 20th 1853, p1.

'The Potato Disease', The Illustrated London News., Oct. 18th 1845.

Thrift's Genealogical Abstracts. Bundle 17, Nos. 3937-4343, Bundle 10, nos. 4344-5029, File 4613, Evatt, Parish of Magheross, Townland of Dromed Itra, National Archives of Ireland.

Whelan, Kevin. *The Atlas of the Irish Rural Landscape*, Cork University Press, 1997.

Whelan, Kevin. *Pre and Post-Famine Landscape Change*, in The Great Irish Famine, ed. Cathal Póirtéir, RTE/Mercier Press, 1995.

Wood-Martin, William Gregory. 'Traces of the elder faiths in Ireland: a folklore sketch: a handbook of Irish pre-Christian traditions', 1902.

NEWSPAPER ARTCLES:

South Wexford Agricultural Society
-London Times, Nov 30th 1829, p8.

Kelly's Horticultural Career:
-Freemans Journal, April 24th, 1828, p1.
-Freemans Journal, August 16th, 1828, p1.
-Freemans Journal, June 9th, 1829, p1.
-Freemans Journal, August 11th, 1829, p2.
-Freemans Journal, August 17th, 1829; p1.
-Freemans Journal, June 17th, 1835, p2.
-Freemans Journal, April 22nd, 1836, p3.
-The Farmer's Gazette and Journal of Practical Horticulture October 3rd, 1846, p360.
-The Farmer's Gazette and Journal of Practical Horticulture November 28th, 1846, p490.
-The Farmer's Gazette and Journal of Practical Horticulture December 26th, 1846, p547.
-Dublin Evening Post, April 20th, 1847.
-The United Irishman, February 19th, 1848, p13.
-Dublin Weekly Nation, February 16th, 1850, p14.
-The Farmer's Gazette and Journal of Practical Horticulture November 1st, 1851, p526.
-The Farmer's Gazette and Journal of Practical Horticulture, November 8th, 1851, p535.
-Freemans Journal, April 27th, 1852, p4.
-The Farmer's Gazette and Journal of Practical Horticulture, March 19th, 1853, p16.
-The Farmer's Gazette and Journal of Practical Horticulture, March 26th, 1853, p152-153
-The Farmer's Gazette and Journal of Practical Horticulture November 26th, 1853, p.587.
-The Farmer's Gazette and Journal of Practical Horticulture, April 2nd, 1859, p98.
-Dublin Evening Post, July 31st, 1868, p4.

Portrane Valuation:
-Leinster Express, 21st August 1841, p3.

Kelly on crops:
-Leinster Express, 12th December 1846, p4.
-Anglo-Celt, 5th May 1847, p4.
-The Farmer's Gazette and Journal of Practical Horticulture, August 2nd, 1856, p11.

Sophia Evans' generosity during the famine:
-London Express, November 24th 1849,

Kelly v. Evans game preservation case:
-Freemans Journal, Dec. 22nd 1870; p5.
-Leinster Express Jan. 7th 1871; p4.

Kelly v. Evans land improvement case:
-Freemans Journal, Wed. May 14th 1873; p7.

Maurice Butterly vs Sir Charles Domville
-Leinster Express July 1st, 1871; p7.

Death of George Evans.
-Freemans Journal, July 04, 1842; p2.

Death of Joshua Evans.
-Dublin Daily Express, January 22nd, 1864, p1.

Rogerstown Embankment Affair:
-Evening Freeman. 28 November 28th,1861, p.1
-The Farmer's Gazette and Journal of Practical Horticulture, Dec. 21st 1861, pp.19-20
-Freemans Journal, January 9th, 1862, p1.
-Evening Freeman, January 11th 1862, p1.
-Freemans Journal, February 7th, 1862, p1.

Kelly's Life & Death in Portrane.
-Freemans Journal, March 18th 1859; p1.
-Freemans Journal July 8th, 1859; p3.
-Freemans Journal, June 16th 1870; p1.
-Freemans Journal, March 7th, 1881, p1.
-Dublin Daily Express, April 9th, 1881, p8.
-Nation Sat. October 22nd 1881; p18.

Kelly's political life:

-Freemans Journal, January 1st, 1873; p6.
-Irish Times, January 24th, 1873, p2.
-Nation, April 11th 1874, p2.
-Freemans Journal, October 13th, 1874; p.6
-Dundalk Democrat January 23rd,1875; p7.
-Freemans Journal, April 16th, 1875; p9
-Freemans Journal, May 12th, 1875, p2.
-Nation, May 22nd 1875; p2.
-Freemans Journal, October 19th, 1875; p2.
-Freeman's Journal, January 3rd, 1876; p6.
-Freemans Journal, February 1st, 1876; p4.
-Freemans Journal, March 15th, 1876; p.2
-Freemans Journal, July 21st 1877; p6.
-Nation, December 1st, 1877; p12.
-Nation, December 22nd, 1877; p5.
-Freemans Journal, January 18th, 1878; p5.
-Nation, February 2nd 1878; p3.
-Freemans Journal, March 9th, 1878; p3.
-Nation, March 16th 1878; p3.
-Nation, June 21st, 1879; Page: 7
-Nation October 25th, 1879; p5
-Dublin Weekly Nation, Jan 31st 1880, p5
-Nation Sat. February 7th 1880; p15
-Irish Times, February 28th, 1880, p6
-Freemans Journal, March 6th, 1880 p7.
-Freemans Journal, April 3rd, 1880 p4.
-Freemans Journal, April 17th, 1880 p3.
-Dublin Weekly Nation, July 24th 1880, p4.
-Freemans Journal, August 18th, 1880 p2.
-Freemans Journal, August 25th, 1880 p2.

MANUSCRIPT SOURCES

Poor law records of Balrothery Union, 1844-1921, National Archives, Dublin. MFGS/49/29-31; Balrothery Poor Law Union Board-Guardians Minute Books:

-A13 Nov 1851 to Aug 1852, folio 9, Item 5, page 517:
-A23 May 1857 to Oct 1857, folio 11, item 3, page 299.
-A24 Oct 1857 to Apr 1858, folio 9, item 4, page 263.
-A24 Oct 1857 to Apr 1858, folio 14, item 4, page 284.
-A32 Oct 1861 to Apr 1862, folio 9, item 4, page 153.
-A41 Apr 1866 to Sep 1866, folio 15, item 4, page 95.
-A45 Mar 1868 to Sep 1868, folio 15, item 8, page 47.
-A45 May 1857 to Oct 1857, folio 11, item 3, page 299.
-A47 Mar 1869 to Sep 1869, folio 15, item 2, page 47.
-A49 Mar 1870 to Oct 1870, folio 15, item 4, page 47.
-A50 Sep 1870 to Apr 1871, folio 15, item 5, page 431.
-A52 Oct 1871 to Apr 1872, folio 9, item 7, page 409.
-A54 Nov 1872 to May 1873, folio 15, item 2, page 335.
-A56 Nov 1873 to May 1874, folio 15, item 4, page 287.
-A58 Dec 1874 to Jul 1875, folio 13, item 6, page 221.
-A60 Jan 1876 to Jul 1876, folio 13, item 2, page 157.
-A62 Feb 1877 to Aug 1877, folio 13, item 4, page 125.
-A64 Mar 1878 to Sep 1878, folio 13, item 6, page 61.
-A65 Sep 1878 to Mar 1879, folio 10, item 7, page 42.
-A66 Mar 1879 to Sep 1879, folio 13, item 1, page 13.

National Archives, Wills Register 1858-1900, William Nolan, Grant of Probate, 1878/1878/1876, p56-57, http://census.nationalarchives.ie/reels/wr/007604261_00058.pdf

St. James' Dublin. Catholic Parish Registers. Book Number 2, page 95, entry no. 1521, record identifier. DU-RC-BA-332482. via www.irishgenealogy.ie.

St. Mary's Dublin, Catholic Parish Registers, Vol 3; 17th Sept. 1836, National Library of Ireland, 09159/03.

ILLUSTRATIONS BY CHAPTER

INTRODUCTION

- Potato Field. Public Domain. Image by Orhan Can from Pixabay. Link - https://pixabay.com/photos/potato-potato-pictures-potatoes-3429379/

THE BANNOW FARM SCHOOL

- Bannow Farm School photographs, courtesy of the National Inventory of Architectural Heritage

FROM FARMHILL TO PORTRANE

- The Evans Estate Portrane © Gerard Ronan
- Chalk Sunday in the county of Kilkenny, image courtesy of Illustrated London News Ltd/Mary Evans

KELLY'S FAMINE BREAD

- Large group of Irish Peasants, by Detroit Publishing Company, Courtesy of Library of Congress, Reproduction Number: LC-USZ62-31651, Call Number: LOT 3107, no. 51.
- Blighted Potato. Public Domain, via Wikimedia Commons...https://commons.wikimedia.org/w/index.php?curid=232492
- Mangelwurzel, from Wikimedia Commons (no restrictions) ...https://upload.wikimedia.org/wikipedia/commons/1/19/Farm_and_garden_annual_%2815766085834%29.jpg

SOUP AND SALVATION

- Irish Famine. Public Domain via Wikimedia Commons. Link...https://upload.wikimedia.org/wikipedia/commons/d/d4/Famine.jpg
- Potato Famine. Courtesy of Samuel Austin [CC BY-SA 3.0 (https://creativecommons.org/licenses/by-sa/3.0)] via Wikimedia Commons.
- Glasnevin Cemetery. Public Domain. by TuendeBede from Pixabay...https://pixabay.com/photos/glasnevin-dublin-ireland-cemetery-2691261/

THE IRISH SMALL FARMER OF 1847

- Clydesdales. Public Domain. By Jessie Rockeman from Pixabay. https://pixabay.com/photos/clydesdale-plowing-horse-1106337/
- Cover of Irish Small Farmer of 1847, by William Kelly, The Farmers' Journal, 1847
- Lazy Beds. Public Domain. Image by Wolfgang Ehrecke from Pixabay. https://pixabay.com/photos/agriculture-potato-crop-field-2654157/

ACROSS THE ATLANTIC!

- Irish family in front of peasant house, by Detroit Publishing Company. Call Number/Physical Location LOT 3107, no. 52. Repository Library of Congress Prints and Photographs Division Digital Id cph 3a32195 //hdl.loc.gov/loc.pnp/cph.3a32195. Library of Congress Control Number 201765633

THE GARDENERS' REVOLT

- Hyacinth and Letter, image by Pezibear from Pixabay. https://pixabay.com/photos/letters-old-letter-handwriting-font-772504/

A FRESH START

- Family being evicted by landlord c1879. Public Domain, https://commons.wikimedia.org/w/index.php?curid=45953
- Middlefield circa 1975. © Gordon Henderson.

THE MARY JANES OF MIDDLEFIELD

- William Kelly's house at Middlefield © Gerard Ronan
- Middlefield circa 1961 © Gordon Henderson.

THE ROGERSTOWN EMBANKMENT AFFAIR

- Photographs of Balrothery Workhouse and Rogerstown Estuary © Gerard Ronan
- Bladderwrack, image by Dr. Georg Wietschorke from Pixabay. Public Domain. Link – https://pixabay.com/images/search/bladderwrack/
- Garrett's Seeding Drill. Image courtesy of Grace's Guide to British Industrial History
- Turvey Woods © Gerard Ronan

THE DISPENSARY COMMITTEE

- "Anxious moments": Oil painting attributed to John Whitehead Walton, 1894. Credit: Wellcome Library, London.images@wellcome.ac.uk. http://wellcomeimages.org. Copyrighted work available under Creative Commons Attribution only licence CC BY 4.0 http://creativecommons.org/licenses/by/4.0/

LAND AND LAW

- Justice, by Alberto Sanchez, Public domain via https://pixabay.com/photos/justice-statue-dublin-ireland-626461/

AT LAST – A WEDDING

- Wedding Ring. Image by Marina Voitik from Pixabay. https://pixabay.com/photos/hands-ring-hand-fingers-2705251/

HOME RULE

- Isaac Butt by John Butler Yeats. Public Domain, via Wikimedia Commons.
- https://commons.wikimedia.org/wiki/File:Portrait_of_Isaac_Butt.jpg
- Cardinal Cullen, Public Domain via Wikimedia Commons https://commons.wikimedia.org/wiki/File:CardinalPaulCullen.jpg

PARNELL

- Charles Stewart Parnell, by Unknown. Publisher: Currier & Ives, Nassau St., New York, c 1881. United States Library of Congress's Prints and Photographs division under the digital ID cph.3b49969.

THE LAND LEAGUE

- Michael Davitt By Napoleon Sarony. Library of Congress, Public Domain, via Wikimedia Commons https://commons.wikimedia.org/w/index.php?curid=16402841
- The eviction: J.T. Foley, Publisher, 117 Nassau Street, New York, c1871, Library of Congress http://www.loc.gov/pictures/item/2004669163/.

THE LAND LEAGUE (continued).

- Gladstone and the Land League, Public Domain, via https://commons.wikimedia.org/wiki/File:Gladstone_and_Land_League.jpg

BACK TO THE GARDEN

- William Kelly's headstone inscription © Gerard Ronan
- William Kelly's monument © Gerard Ronan

A CURIOUS EXHUMATION!

- Mary Jane Kelly's final resting place. © Gerard Ronan.

INDEX

BY THE SAME AUTHOR...

The Irish Zorro: The Extraordinary Adventures of William Lamport

GERARD RONAN

'Ronan's book is not only an excellent history book, it is a great read. Thoroughly recommended.'

Peter Berresford Ellis. *Irish Democrat*

'Sometimes, historical biography can be a dry read. Ronan's is anything but. He provides interesting insights into the lives of large Irish enclaves in France and Spain in the first half of the 17th century along with harrowing ones of those accused of heresy and subjected to the *auto da fe* of the Inquisition. Ronan's passion and sympathy for his subject shines through so it reads like a novel. A "must-read" for the new year.'

Ann Dunne. *Irish Independent*

'The life and adventures of this pirate, heretic and spy were stranger than any fiction.'

Bookworm. *History Ireland*

ISBN-10: 086322329X
ISBN-13: 978-0863223297

Sophia Parnell-Evans: Feminism, Politics and Farming in 19th Century Portrane

GERARD RONAN

Sophia Parnell-Evans (1780-1853) ran a large and successful farming enterprise at a time when few women had done so. She met two Queens, the ex-wife of Napoleon and knew the radical feminist Margaret Mount Cashel. An friend of both the Darwin and Condorcet families, she was daughter and sister to three of the most prominent Irish politicians of her day, and wife to another.

A radical thinker in her own right, Sophia founded two primary schools in Donabate and had helped in no small way to mitigate the effects of the Great Famine in her locality. The memorial round tower she built in memory of her devoted husband, the MP George Evans, revived a tradition of tower building that had lain dormant for seven centuries. As the great aunt of Charles Stewart Parnell, she even made it into the pages of Joyce's "Finnegan's Wake" as the practical joker "greataunt Sophy".

ISBN-10 : 1999973879
ISBN-13 : 978-1999973872

Margaret Evans: Poet of Portrane

GERARD RONAN

In 1798, Margaret Evans' husband, Hampden, was sentenced to hang for high treason. When his sentence was subsequently commuted to voluntary exile, she was forced to follow him to Hamburg and later to Paris, where she coped with her enforced exile and family tragedies by writing poetry for herself, her daughters and her female friends. Her writing affords us a very personal glimpse of her life as the wife of a leading United Irishman, and also the safe female space that 18th and 19th century women found in the writing and sharing of poetry. Margaret and Hampden Evans played a prominent role in the history of Portrane, and of the United Irishmen, but little was known of their story until now, or indeed of Margaret's poetry.

ISBN-10 : 1999973860
ISBN-13 : 978-1999973865

The Round Towers of Fingal: Their Hidden History

GERARD RONAN

From tolerant Vikings to ambitious Huguenot's, feminist atheists to cultural pressure groups, the story of Fingal's round towers mirrors the development of the complex Irish identity. The men and women who built and restored these towers link them to multiple invasions as well as to Robinson Crusoe, the Book of Kells and Frankenstein. This book will change the way you look at these monuments forever.

ISBN-10: 1999973836
ISBN-13: 978-1999973834

www.ingramcontent.com/pod-product-compliance
Ingram Content Group UK Ltd.
Pitfield, Milton Keynes, MK11 3LW, UK
UKHW020226250726
13967UKWH00001B/218